SUPER CHEAP NEW ZEALAND

The Ultimate Travel Guide for Budget Travelers, Backpackers, Campers, Students and Families

Matthew Baxter

Help spread the word!
Please help this self-published book by writing a review on the website where you bought the book, sharing the book on Facebook, Twitter or Instagram, or telling a friend. As this is a self-funded indie project, it would be super useful and very much appreciated!

Like or follow us to get the latest tips and deals
Join or follow Super Cheap Guides to get the latest information on new discounts and deals, plus interesting budget travel reports. You can also head to the website to read all the latest information or get it sent straight to your inbox by signing up for the free newsletter.

 **www.supercheapguides.com**

 **@SuperCheapGuides**

 **@SuperCheapGuides**

 **@SuperCheapGuide**

Super Cheap Guides
9 Eashing Lane
Godalming, Surrey GU7 2JZ
www.supercheapguides.com/contact/

Book Layout ©2019 BookDesignTemplates.com

Super Cheap New Zealand: The Ultimate Travel Guide for Budget Travelers, Backpackers, Campers, Students and Families / Matthew Baxter - 1st ed.
Paperback ISBN 978-1-913114-05-3
Ebook ISBN 978-1-913114-06-0

Contents

Welcome to New Zealand

Living at the extreme in Queenstown

Welcome to New Zealand, your escape from the hustle and bustle of daily life and a perfect place to unwind, and explore. It's a country of kind, open and laid-back people, with a high standard of living and great weather. New Zealand can also become an expensive place, though, with all that's on offer, from exhilarating skydiving in Queenstown to chilled-out lake cruises at Milford Sound. But there is no need to worry, as with this guide you'll find out how to really enjoy it all on a reasonable budget.

While prices may be higher than some countries due to New Zealand being far away from anywhere else, visitors can still find great deals for everything from food to accommodation. Cheap supermarkets, dollar stores and free water bottle refill spots, among other ways, can be used to keep costs down. And never forget the friendly locals, who are always more than willing to help you out, whether it's giving you a free ride in their car or a cheap night's sleep at their house. So, book that flight and you're sure to have the time of your life!

A little bit of history

The first people to settle here were the ancestors of the Maori people. It is believed that they arrived around 1200 AD, eventually spreading out across the land that they called Aotearoa. Many years later Europeans started to arrive in New Zealand, firstly the Dutch. Explorer Abel Tasman, whom the Tasman Sea is named after, came in 1642. The lands were given the name Nieuw Zeeland by a Dutch mapmaker, after the province of Zeeland in the Netherlands. More than 100 years later, British explorer James Cook arrived on the first of three visits. Then, towards the end of the 18th century European whalers started to come on a regular basis, and by the early 19th century some Europeans had started to build settlements.

In 1840 the Treaty of Waitangi was signed, which gave the British sovereignty over New Zealand. It hasn't all been plain sailing, though, with various rebellions and demonstrations over the years concerning the treatment of Maori people. These days New Zealand is constantly on the change, a diverse mix of cultures, all living in one small country.

How to save on your holiday with this book

Things to do

With this book you'll be shown plenty of options for free things to do, as well as information on available discounts or deals on offer. Try to do the cheaper or free activities first, then if you feel you need to do more, try the more expensive activities in the area. For example, you may find that after doing a free hike up a mountain, joining an expensive zipline tour on the same mountain just isn't worth it. If you still want to try that zipline tour, though, this book will show the best ways to do it on the cheap!

Sample itineraries and discount passes

With all the options available in New Zealand, it can be a bit bewildering to plan your trip. Super Cheap New Zealand will provide sample itineraries for various lengths of stay and for different types of tourists. They are designed to be useable with the discount bus passes or by those who will have their own vehicle. This book will also compare bus passes, rental companies and other options so that you can plan in both a cheap and stress-free way.

Maps designed for budget travelers

Maps are provided to help you get around, with handy icons to show you exactly where all the cheap shops, inexpensive restaurants, discount stores and more are located. Landmark buildings and major hotels have also been included to aid in navigating around. A plus is that most of these landmarks have toilets if needed, plus some have free water fountains, which can be used to refill your water bottle and save on the cost of drinks. You can also save on transportation by using the recommended walking routes.

Map Legend

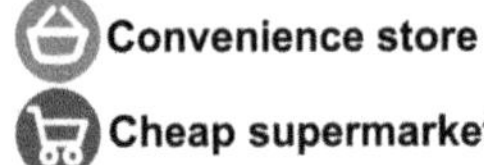

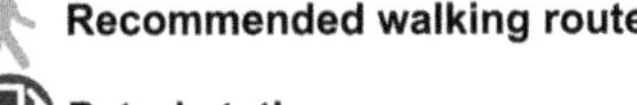

Petrol station

Budget accommodation

Parking

Budget food and drinks

There are plenty of places in New Zealand where you can get a cheap meal for around $6-$10. This book will show you exactly where to find these kinds of prices, which are often hard to find as they may not be on the main shopping streets or only known to locals.

Cooking on your own is a great way to save on costs. The cheapest supermarket chain in New Zealand is PAK'nSAVE, which is similar to American chain Costco in terms of size and batch discounts (no membership fees required though!). Countdown and New World are the main medium-sized supermarket chains. Both have free-to-join member card schemes that offer excellent discounts and just take a minute or two to register for in their stores (New World has a special one for travelers on a short visit). Four Square operates in more rural towns, with slightly higher prices and a smaller selection than in the city. Finally, convenience stores tend to be pricey in New Zealand, so try to avoid them if you can. All these types of stores and directions or maps showing how to get to them are included in this book.

Tap water is drinkable in New Zealand, so fill up your water bottle before heading out for the day. There is a national drive to put refill points across the country, so many places also have free refill taps around town, which are included on the maps in this book.

Recommended budget accommodation

There are several choices for accommodation if you are looking to save big on one of traveling's biggest costs. The 'Budget accommodation in New Zealand' section will summarize the different types and methods you can use to sleep on the cheap. Each relevant destination chapter will then provide recommendations, including those that are part of hostel groups such as YHA or BBH, so it's easy to know which one to sign up with.

Free wifi locations

Free public wifi is available in Auckland, Wellington, Rotorua and Dunedin, as well as in an increasing number of tourist towns, some tourist information centers and all public libraries. Access and speeds can be unreliable, even in major tourist hotspots such as Queenstown, so this book includes instructions and tips on how to get access to free wifi in such places.

New Zealand's top five spots

1) Queenstown

New Zealand's adventure capital is surrounded by snow-capped mountains that many consider to be more beautiful than the Swiss Alps. The town itself is quite large, so it has all the cheap shops, hostels and restaurants that you'll need for your budget holiday.

2) Milford Sound

The country's most popular tourist spot has rightly made a name for itself, with mesmerizing grand cliffs, huge waterfalls and a chance to see dolphins, fur seals and penguins. A bunch of companies are competing to offer cruises here, so deals are numerous.

3) Mount Cook

Full of hiking tracks for all abilities, Mount Cook is a splendid place to go if you need to get away from it all. There are no chain stores here, it's all about getting back to nature.

4) Franz Josef

Stunning glacier that needs to be visited before it all melts away! There are a variety of walks and hikes near the glacier, passing some pristine forests, ice-melt streams and grand valleys. It's a bit of a journey to get there, but it's well worth the effort.

5) Auckland

New Zealand's biggest city has a lot to offer, with cheap volcanic island day trips, delicious hawker markets and many free festivals. Plus there's super tasty wine on Waiheke Island!

Map of New Zealand

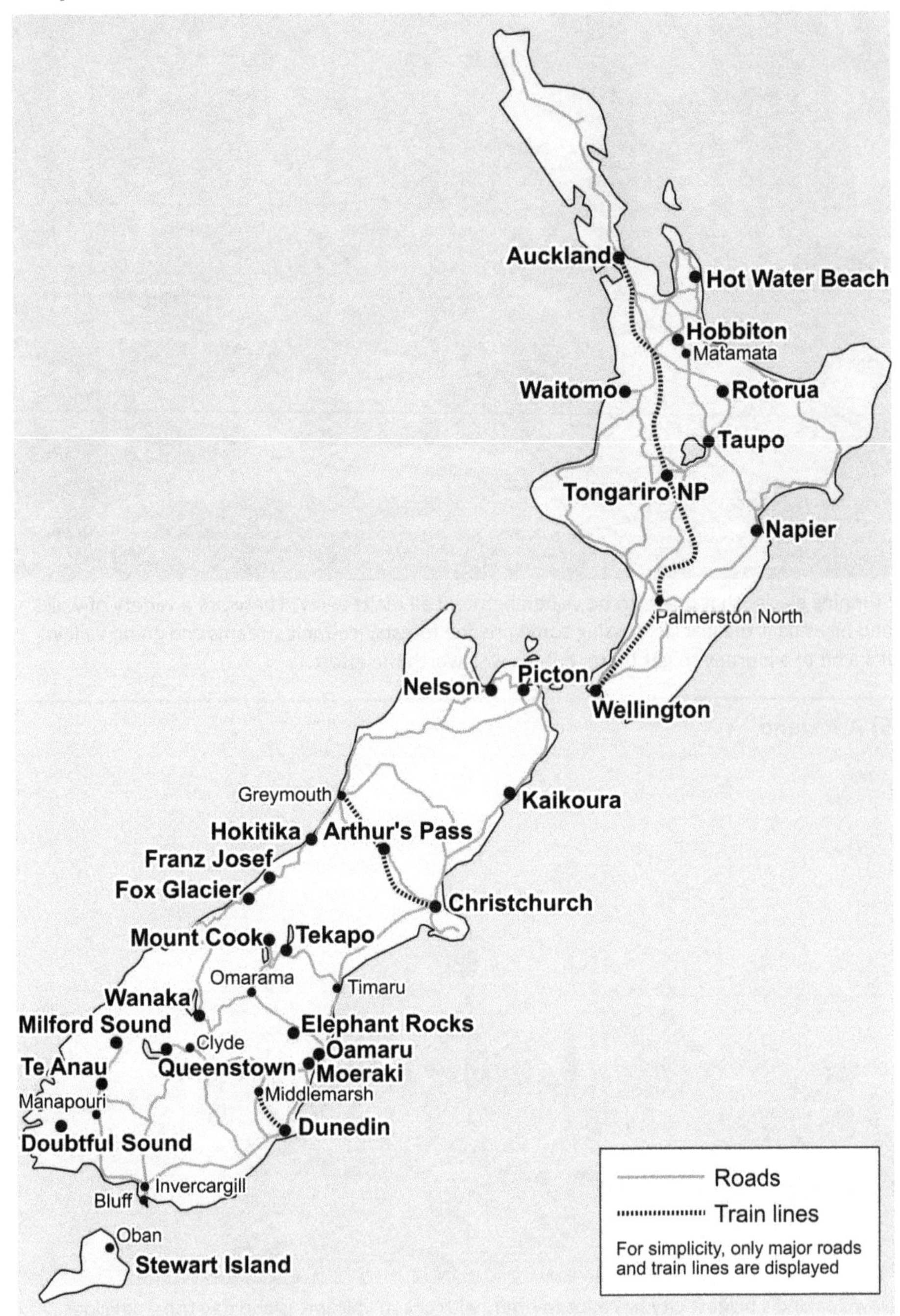

When to go to New Zealand

Springtime in Queenstown

The seasons in New Zealand are the opposite to what most visitors are accustomed to. Be sure to check www.supercheapguides.com and the Met Service for the latest weather forecasts.

Spring (September to November)

A lovely time to come to see the blossoms and beautiful native flowers. With all the snow and ice melting from the winter, the waterfalls at places such as Milford Sound can also be bigger.

Summer (December to February)

This is a perfect time to hit the beaches, cool off at the lakes on your road trip or head out for a hike. Prices are higher, but everywhere will be open apart from the ski resorts.

Fall/Autumn (March to May)

With more settled weather than other seasons, this could be the best time to visit. It's a great time to go hiking, as you'll escape the summer crowds and probably won't have to worry about snow or ice. Cycling and kayaking are also popular pursuits at this time of the year.

Winter (June to August)

Bring a thick winter coat, as it can get really chilly here, especially on the South Island. Come for a spot of snowboarding or skiing, or stay in the cities and towns and save a load of money on the low-season prices.

Peak seasons to avoid

The peak season tends to be late December to early March, when prices can increase quite a bit due to all the Brits and Americans coming here to escape their winters. Apart from this period, try to avoid the Easter holidays and around Christmas.

Hiking in New Zealand

Walking through the first section of the Milford Track, one of the Great Walks

Taking a hike or walk in New Zealand's forests and mountains is a highlight for many tourists. Due to the country's remote location, the plants and wildlife you'll see and hear may be completely different to what you are used to. There are countless easy-to-follow tracks all over the country, and you'll never be too far from one. Below are some of the best for budget travelers here on a short holiday, but if you are looking for more challenging, multi-day hikes then consider doing one of the Department of Conservation's Great Walks (www.doc.govt.nz). Cheap mountain huts and transportation options are available on their website. Book early to avoid disappointment.

Top places to hike in New Zealand

1) Mount Cook

Several tracks start from the settlement itself that cater to all kinds of abilities, with amazing mountain views and lots of cheap accommodation.

2) Arthur's Pass

A quiet spot for a walk or hike, plus there's also a high chance of seeing the playful kea birds. You'll never have your experience affected by noisy tour groups at this super peaceful area.

3) Te Anau

A convenient place to stock up on food and equipment before a hike, Te Anau is near both the Kepler and popular Milford tracks. There are also easier walks you can start from the town.

4) Tongariro Alpine Crossing

The oldest national park in New Zealand and also a World Heritage area, Tongariro is full of dramatic volcanic landscapes, native beech forests and huge glacial valleys.

5) Queenstown

This big town has a gondola for those that want to skip the ascent up one of its biggest hills, plus many other tracks that are a short drive or bus ride away.

Winter sports in New Zealand

New Zealand is an excellent country to go for snowboarding, skiing or other winter sports. With resorts all over the country, especially in the mountains of the South Island, tourists really are spoilt for choice. Costs can add up though, so follow the tips below and book as early as you can.

How to save money on winter sports

Early bird passes

Get up to 60% off when you buy a season pass at many resorts before their early bird deadlines (usually February or March). Getting one of these means you'll usually start to save money after a week or so, compared to buying day tickets or multi-day passes.

Avoid the peak season

The peak season runs around mid-July to the end of August, so try to visit in June or September. The snow may not be as good, but many resorts have cheaper tickets and the slopes are not as busy with school children on their holidays.

Skip the expensive resort restaurants

The restaurants at most resorts are very pricey, so bring along your own food and drink to significantly cut down on costs. Some resorts, such as Cardrona near Queenstown, even have boiling water taps, so you can just bring some cup noodles with you!

Rent or buy your gear outside the resorts

You don't want to arrive at a resort and be forced to pay big just to rent some skis for a day. Shop around in town for cheaper rentals away from the official resort offices, and consider buying secondhand equipment, which will save you even more if you're staying a while.

Other discounts

Some car rental companies, such as Omega, and backpacker groups, such as YHA, will offer discounts to their customers for ski resorts and winter activities. Some ski resorts also give better deals if you book online, rather than in person at the resort.

Top resorts in New Zealand

Here are some of the best options for first timers to New Zealand. The prices listed below are the standard ones, so remember that you'll receive heavy discounts when booking well in advance or booking multi-day tickets rather than just one day. Opening times vary wildly based on the current weather and the scheduled opening, so always check the resort's official website before booking or making your way there.

NZSki Resorts

NZSki run three resorts, two near Queenstown (The Remarkables and Coronet Peak) and one near Christchurch (Mount Hutt). While their passes can look pricey at first, you can really start to save by visiting all the resorts together as a package, plus you'll be able to enjoy a large variety of slopes. All the resorts have runs for any level of ability. Coronet Peak is particularly well suited for intermediate skiers and snowboarders, but can get pretty crowded at points. The Remarkables has mind-blowing scenery, but snowfall is said to be inconsistent. Finally, Mount Hutt has more reliable snow and a decent self-serve restaurant, but the ride up is daunting at best, and quite scary at worse, with occasional closures.

3 Peaks Season Pass: adults $1199, children $599, seniors $699, students $699. Day pass: adults $119-129, children $59-69, seniors $59-69, students $79-95. Night pass: adults $65, children $45, seniors $45 • www.nzski.com *• Regular shuttle buses from Queenstown, Christchurch and Methven (town near Mount Hutt)*

Cardrona

Owned by Real Journeys, who also run many tours in Queenstown and the Fiordland National Park, Cardrona is considered by many locals to be better than the NZSki resorts (with some locals joking that Coronet Peak should be called Concrete Peak!). It has slopes for all kinds of skiers and snowboarders, with particularly good facilities and infrastructure for beginners.

Unlimited Season Pass: adults $1299, children $499, seniors $799, students $899 (Saver season passes available when booking early). Day pass: adults $120, children $62, seniors $90, students $97 • www.cardrona.com *• Regular shuttle buses from Queenstown or Wanaka*

Treblecone

Located near the lakeside town of Wanaka, Treblecone is the largest ski resort on the South Island. The number of slopes for beginners is not as good as elsewhere (only around 10% is for beginners), so Treblecone is best for experienced snowboarders and skiers willing to pay extra for such good snow. Prices are quite high for adults, but savings can be made if your group includes young children and seniors.

Season Pass: adults $1999, children $599 (under 5 FREE), seniors $999 (over 80 FREE). Day pass: adults $149, children $75. • www.treblecone.com *• Free shuttle bus from Wanaka twice a day in the mornings*

Whakapapa

An easy choice if you're based in Auckland, this very family-friendly resort has a large number of slopes for beginners and a big area for the children to learn the basics. With dozens of runs, you'll no doubt be able to spend at least a few days here. Just note that it can get crowded on weekends, so avoid then if possible.

Season Pass: adults $1299, youth (5-17 years old) $779, child (with accompanying adult) $325, under 5 FREE. Day pass: adults $119-129, children $59-69, seniors $59-69, students $79-95 • www.mtruapehu.com *• Shuttle buses available from National Park, Taupo and Turangi*

Festivals and events

Haka, the traditional Maori dance

Here is a list of the most famous and popular yearly festivals and events in New Zealand, which will help you to decide where to go and when to come here. For more events, check Eventfinda (www.eventfinda.co.nz), which lists thousands across the country and for almost any day of the year. If in Auckland, also check out the Silo Park on the waterfront (www.silopark.co.nz), which has free events throughout the year, especially in summer.

One annoyance with festivals in New Zealand can be that many of them charge pretty high entrance fees, so avoid these if you can. For example, if you see a beer festival charging $20 to enter, just spend that money in the local craft beer bars instead! All the following festivals are free to enter or cost just a few dollars to get in.

January

Late January Birdman, Wellington: See all sorts of crazy people at the waterfront, dressed up as planes and birds, attempting to fly as far as they can from the pier. All very silly!
Late January SeePort Festival, Auckland: One of Auckland's biggest free festivals, this one celebrates the city's rich maritime history. There are loads of places selling cheap food, games for the children to play and fireworks in the evenings.
January or February (depends on Chinese calendar) Lantern Festival, Auckland Domain: Stunning displays of oriental lanterns, as well as traditional performances and food to try out. Located at the park just outside the Auckland War Memorial Museum.

February

6th Te Ra o Waitangi, Wellington: Celebrate Waitangi Day with traditional haka dance performances, plus Maori music and story-telling shows. You can also try out Maori food and take part in traditional Maori games at this event in Waitangi Park.
6th International Kai Festival, Nelson: Experience New Zealand's indigenous culture, as well as sample the local food and wine. Located at the Founders Heritage Park.
Around 19th January Wellington Pasifika Festival: Experience all the sounds and flavors, enjoy some free activities and learn about the Pacific communities in New Zealand.

March

Early March Hokitika Wildfoods Festival: Try out all the unique and crazy food that New Zealand has to offer, from whitebait fritters, to huhu grubs (beetles), to mountain oysters.
Mid to late March Auckland Arts Festival: Everything you could imagine, from local opera to street performers. Many of the events are free and some cater to children too.

April

25th ANZAC Day Dawn Service, Auckland: A very special day for all New Zealanders, ANZAC Day commemorates the county's fallen soldiers. Held outside the Auckland War Memorial Museum, thousands come to pay their tributes, with music and poetry in the museum afterwards.

May

Early May Seafood Fest, Coromandel Town: Stuff yourself on all kinds of fresh local fish.
Mid-May Christchurch Food Festival: 70,000 plus visitors from across the world come to try Christchurch's local culinary delights.
Late May to early June Steampunk Festival, Oamaru: Everyone in town gets dressed up in their steampunk-style costumes, making for a rather novel festival.

June

Mid to late June Queenstown Winter Festival: Live music on the waterfront, comedy shows and fireworks in the evening. Also has a dog derby and dog barking event!
Mid to late June Matariki Festival: Celebrate the Maori New Year with various events, from cooking demonstrations to singing and dancing performances. A large cluster of events are held in Wellington and Auckland, but smaller towns also hold events.

July to August

Now's not the time to stay in town for a festival! Head to the ski slopes and see what's on. Most major ski resorts have events throughout the winter, so check the website of the place you're going to and see what's on. Queenstown tends to be best, with Coronet Peak, The Remarkables and Cardrona having a few events each season.

September

Late September Otahuhu Food Festival, Auckland: Huge food festival that fills the streets of this suburb near central Auckland.
Late September to early October Alexandra Blossom Festival: Located a short drive away from Queenstown in the South Island, Alexandra is a fantastic place to welcome the spring, with its large parks and various fun events, such as truck and BMX shows, music and a parade through the town center.

October

Mid to late October Nelson Arts Festival: About two weeks of comedy, carnivals, dance, rock music and more in the sunny town of Nelson.

November

Mid-November NZ Irish Fest: A fun celebration for the Irish communities in New Zealand, the Irish Fest has all the classic music, dancing and drinking events that you would expect. The various events are held in Auckland, Wellington and Christchurch.

December

Mid-December Christmas in the Park, Auckland: Free music festival for the festive season, with rides and amusements, plus some food trucks selling cheap food.

Getting to and around New Zealand

How to get there and away

Due to the long distances involved getting to New Zealand, try to be flexible with dates. As well as budget airlines such as Jetstar, Qantas and Air New Zealand also have excellent sales on occasionally, so be sure to check their official websites, as well as grabaseat.co.nz. Some of these deals are exclusive to their newsletter subscribers, so definitely sign up to those too. Check out the chapters for Auckland, Wellington, Christchurch and Queenstown for more information and how to get to and from these international airports.

Getting around by car or campervan

The main international car rental companies have offices across the country, but there are a few local companies that offer better deals. Check out local companies such as Apex, GO and Jucy Rentals, as well as rental comparison websites like www.rentalcars.com and www.skyscanner.net before you go. Some of these local rental companies also offer older cars, for example that have done more than 200,000 kilometers, for extra low prices. Prices for rentals varies a lot, depending on factors such as where you drop off your vehicle, how long you rent it for and what time of the year, but using the price comparison sites helps to simplify things!

Campervans

Campervans are extremely popular for budget travelers in New Zealand, as they cut out the cost of accommodation and allow you to travel almost anywhere. For campervans, also check out the websites of Wicked Campers, Spaceships Rentals and Britz, then download the CamperMate app for the locations where you are allowed to stay the night, often for free.

Buy a vehicle

If you're staying for more than a few weeks, it will probably be cheaper in the end to buy a secondhand vehicle, for example via New Zealand's version of eBay, TradeMe. You can then sell the car at the end of your trip to get some, or if you're lucky, all of your money back! Also remember that you can save even more if you meet fellow travelers on the way who join you, as you can split the cost of gas.

Use a relocation service

Finally, a very welcome new development is the car and campervan relocation sites. For a tiny amount, sometimes as low as $1 a day, various people and companies are looking to get a vehicle of theirs transported to a certain location. If your dates and destinations match up, it's an amazing way to save. Check out www.transfercar.co.nz and www.imoova.com, as well as the car rental companies such as Jucy, to see what's available.

Getting around by bus

If you're not renting or buying a vehicle, getting around on the bus is the most popular way to explore a particular island. There are a few ways to do it, depending on what kind of traveler you are:

InterCity

InterCity is the main bus operator in New Zealand, with a network that goes to almost any main tourist spot on either of the two main islands. They have two passes and a reward program that visitors can use to save money, and you can also just buy individual tickets. These prices can vary from day to day, so the prices in this guide should just be used for reference. Tickets can be as low as $1 if you book more than a few months in advance, in which case it may be cheaper to do individual tickets rather than get a bus pass. Check the InterCity website for exact prices at www.intercity.co.nz, and be sure to click the 'Other fare types' option, as there are sometimes lowers prices for certain travelers, like backpackers or students.

InterCity Rewards

An excellent choice for those who are doing lots of individual tickets, for example if they are staying multiple months. Every time you book a ticket with InterCity, you receive 'Reward dollars' which can then be put towards future trips. One Reward dollar equates to one New Zealand dollar, so it's a simple system to use, and all you need to do is take a few minutes to sign up on their website. Note that you cannot receive Reward dollars when using a bus pass.

FlexiPass

An hours-based bus pass aimed at backpackers and independent travelers. There is no set itinerary, so you can book as you go along. Various lengths are available, so use the booking search function on the InterCity website to compare and see if you'll save money by getting a FlexiPass. It may be that if you are going on routes that are generally expensive, then paying by the hour is cheaper. Passes are valid for 12 months and you are allowed to sell off unused hours at the end. *60 hours: $459. 45 hours: $355. 35 hours: $282. 25 hours: $209. 15 hours: $132*

TravelPass

Based on the most popular routes in New Zealand, this is a good option for first timers to the country. While the routes with the TravelPass are fixed, they cover routes taken by most travelers. Some also include day tours at a discounted rate compared to buying separately. Once you have purchased a pass, all you need to do is log in to the website and select the departure dates and times. *Passes $125 to $1045 • See* www.intercity.co.nz/bus-pass/travelpass *for the current list of passes*

Stray

A well-known operator of hop-on, hop-off buses aimed at backpackers, Stray drives along many different pre-determined routes, which tend to be a little cheaper than the InterCity TravelPass routes. Drivers are a lively bunch of people, always up for a good time and very knowledgeable about the places they visit. They can also arrange accommodation (they have an accommodation guarantee) and get you Stray exclusive discounts on tours, so it's a really hassle-free option for budget travelers. Prices are often discounted, sometimes significantly during winter, so be sure to check www.straytravel.com/special-deals before purchasing a pass. Most passes are valid for 12 months. *National pass: $1495. South Island pass: $895. North Island pass: $625 (various other 'Freestyle' passes available for more specific routes)*

Kiwi Experience

Offers a similar experience to Stray, but has bigger buses and slightly lower prices. They are usually more popular with younger travelers on their gap years, so it may be a bit too much like party central for older travelers. They also have a slightly larger network, additionally reaching Dunedin on the southern island. If these backpacker hop-on, hop-off buses seem like a good fit for you, have a read of this book and decide where you want to go, then check out their websites to see which the best pass is for you. Kiwi Experience also have some great deals from time to time, so have a look at www.kiwiexperience.com/book-your-nz-trip/kiwi-experience-deals. *National passes: $1139-$1689. South Island passes: $699-$999. North Island passes: $299-$769*

Getting around by air

Flying around New Zealand can be a bit hit and miss at times, with prices sometimes too expensive and other times unbelievably cheap. There are two main companies, national carrier Air New Zealand and budget airline Jetstar, but many routes are run exclusively by Air New Zealand, meaning high prices. Jetstar prices can get really low, for example $30-$40 from the capital Wellington to Christchurch, so have a look at various dates on www.skyscanner.net and on the Jetstar official website. Make sure you book as far in advance as you can and use www.grabaseat.co.nz for discounted Air New Zealand flights.

Hitchhiking

New Zealand has to be one of the easiest countries in the world to go hitchhiking. It's really part of the culture here, and for many travelers, and locals, the normal way to get around. Most hostels also have notice boards, where people will put a note to see if anyone wants to join them somewhere, or you can put a note up to see if anyone is going where you want to go and if you can join them.

Additionally, you are more than likely to meet people in hostels going your way too, so never be afraid to ask if you can join them! Carpool apps like CarpoolWorld and Chariot are also worth downloading, but if you just head out onto the pavement and put your hand out, it usually isn't too long before you can get a ride.

Sample itineraries

These itineraries can be done with your own method of transport, or via bus. The advantage with having your own car is that you'll be able to stop off at interesting lakes, parks and so on, but Stray and Kiwi Experience also tend to break up their trips with stops at places of interest. InterCity usually stop only at major destinations and for lunch or dinner breaks. They can also be used to supplement the pass you get with Stray and Kiwi Experience, as they go pretty much anywhere you'll need to go.

South Island highlights (7-10 days)

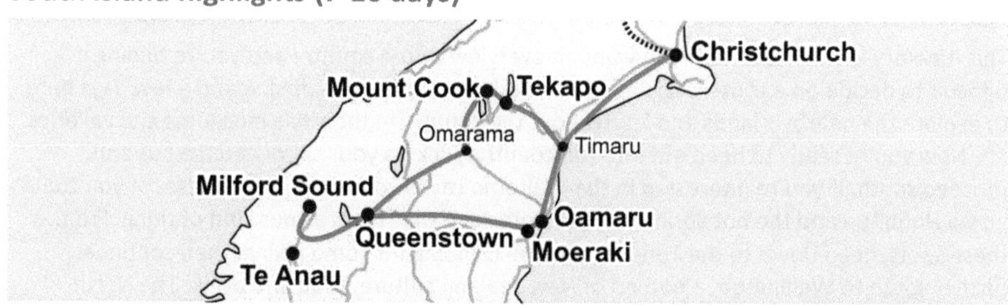

This route could be started in Christchurch or Queenstown, so start at a place that is cheapest to get to. It's a simple, almost circular route that delivers all the South Island's big hitters without backtracking on yourself too much. You'll get to spend some time in beautiful mountain towns like Tekapo, go hiking near Mount Cook, see Victorian heritage buildings in Oamaru and see the famous fjords in Milford Sound. Queenstown is also a great location to spend a few days with all the extreme activities available there, as well as some spectacular walks and hikes.

The classic north to south journey (2-3 weeks)

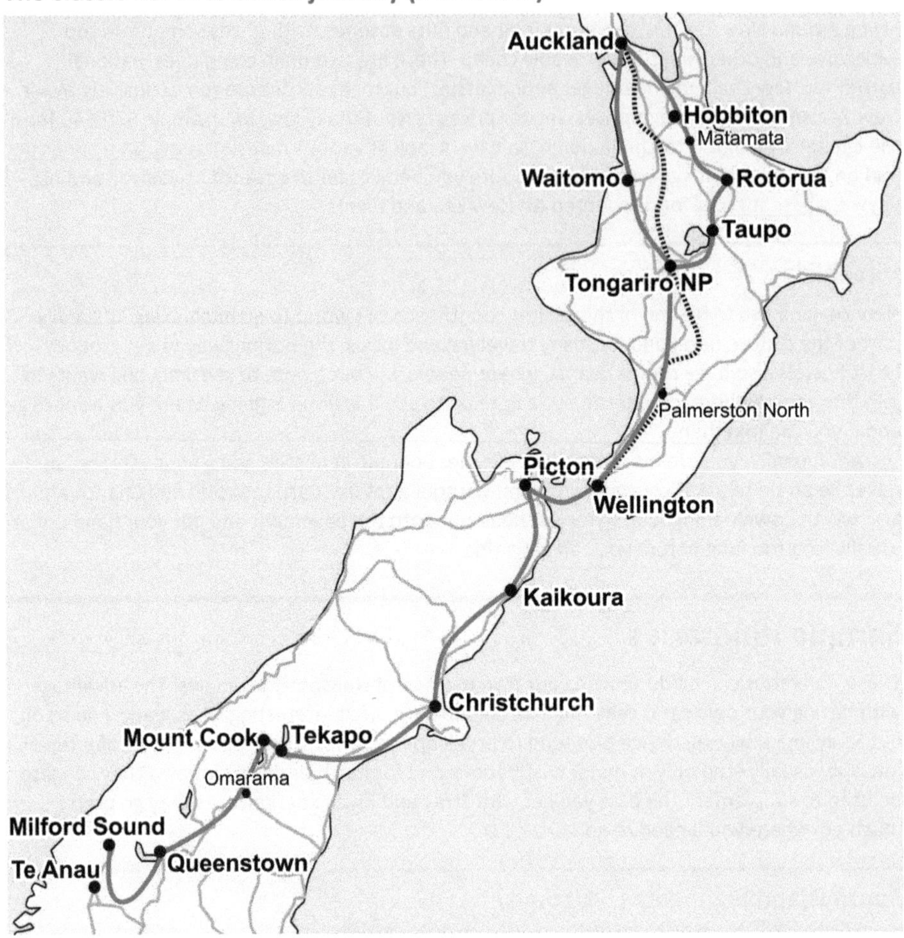

This itinerary is a safe choice if you want an overview of the country and you're finding it difficult to decide on a route. Starting from Auckland in the north, first spend a few days here to explore the nearby islands and learn about the country in the city's museums and galleries.

Now you're ready to head out into the country! Pick up your car or catch a bus and proceed south. If you're interested in the Waitomo caves you could go via these, or you could go via Hobbiton and the hot spring town of Rotorua if that's more your kind of thing. From these spots, head down to the Tongariro Alpine Crossing for some hiking, then continue further south to Wellington, a hotbed of New Zealand culture, food and drink. The North Island should take about one week.

From Wellington, head over to Picton on the ferry and spend a day here chilling out on the beach with a drink or two. Next head down the east coast, stopping off in Kaikoura if you want to see the whales, then down to Christchurch. Spend a day here checking out the art scene and picking up supplies at the discount mega stores.

From Christchurch, continue south, making a turn into the mountains for Tekapo and Mount Cook. More hiking opportunities are on offer here, or you can try the delicious local salmon, so spend a day in each settlement. Next, head to Queenstown and spend a few days here enjoying the extreme activities like skydiving, bungy jumping and jetboating. Finally do a return trip to Milford Sound, ending your trip at the country's most stunning location. When back in Queenstown you could either fly back home from here, or get a cheap flight back to Auckland.

Get away from the crowds on the South Island (around 1 week)

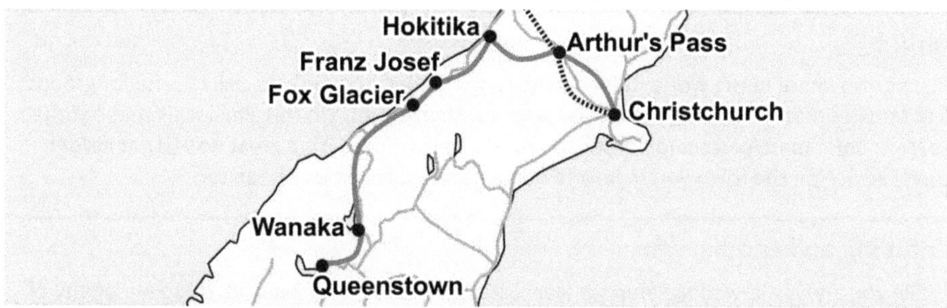

This itinerary can be started in either direction, from Queenstown or Christchurch, which both have international airports offering budget flights. If starting in Queenstown, spend a few days here and start with a bang by jumping out of a plane or bungy jumping off a bridge! Next head up to the west coast, stopping off along the way in Wanaka to relax on the quiet waterfront.

Heading up the west coast, you can check out the grand glaciers of Fox Glacier and Franz Josef over a few days. Next, stop off in Hokitika to stock up on food and enjoy some traditional fish and chips on the beach. From here you can turn east and continue to Arthur's Pass. Here you can really get out into nature and do some lovely hikes and walks in the surrounding national park. Finally, head down to Christchurch, where you can spend any remaining time checking out the museums and street art.

Budget accommodation in New Zealand

Hostels

With beds from around $25 to $35 a night, staying at a hostel, called a 'backpackers' here, is the default option for most budget travelers. These days you're also not just confined to a dorm room, as many hostels have private rooms and family rooms at lower prices than many hotels. They are also a great way to meet fellow travelers.

Backpacker organizations

Existing YHA members should definitely stick to their hostels here, as they receive 10% off accommodation, as well as some discounts on tours. BBH is another hostel group, with similar discounts, as well as 10% off the Interislander and Bluebridge ferries going between the north and south islands. Both groups offer coverage of most tourist spots in the country, but certainly not all. Therefore it's best to first decide which places you want to visit, then see which hostel group offers the biggest selection, and then finally go for the one that will save you most on your trip. Just note that BBH Club Cards cost $35 and YHA cards costs $25 (international YHA cards also accepted), so if buying one you'll need to spend at least a week or so at the group's hostels.

Coachsurfing

Worth trying if you're really stuck for cash, sometimes very kind people will offer a sofa for free on sites like www.couchsurfing.com. Many hosts are keen to meet new people, and as budget travelers too, know how much a free night's sleep can help people out. Make sure you read the reviews for the hosts and follow the safety guidelines on the website.

Airbnb

Just as elsewhere in the world, this website (www.airbnb.com) is especially useful for groups and families that want to book a whole place for themselves. On this site, locals rent out their spare rooms, apartments and houses to tourists to stay in, so it's a great way to get insider travel advice on the town you're in, and bargains can sometimes be had too!

Camping and campervans

While you aren't allowed to camp for free just anywhere in New Zealand, there are plenty of areas where you can park your motorhome or set up your tent free of charge. Free campsites may have basic facilities such as toilets and picnic tables, but facilities can be limited. Head to www.freedomcamping.org or use its Camping NZ and Camper Mate apps for a comprehensive list of campsites and places to park. You can also stop off at a tourist information center or Department of Conservation office and ask for available sites nearby. The Department of Conservation website at www.doc.govt.nz also has a list of campsites on its hiking trails.

WWOOF and working for accommodation

Another excellent way to get free accommodation, especially if doing a working holiday visa, is to volunteer somewhere in exchange for a bed. International organization WWOOF (World Wide Opportunities on Organic Farms) is the first port of call for most people trying this method for the first time. It's a well trusted organization where farms provide accommodation and usually food in exchange for you helping them out for a few hours a day. No experience is usually required, just a good attitude!

There are a few other ways to work for accommodation if a farm doesn't sound like your kind of thing. Many people work as cleaners or receptionists at hostels in exchange for a night's sleep, so if this sounds appealing head to the website of the place where you want to stay and send them an email to see if they need help. Alternatively, an easy website to use is www.workaway.info, but also try searching on the long-established HelpX website at www.helpx.net. These sites provide countless ways to get a free bed, from babysitting to working at organic bakeries and restaurants.

Things to know before you visit New Zealand

Exchange rates

These are the rates as of August 2019. See www.supercheapguides.com for the latest rates.
1 US Dollar = $1.50 • 1 Euro = $1.66 • 1 British Pound = $1.87 • 1 Australian Dollar = $1.09 • 100 yen = $1.38 • 1 Canadian Dollar = $1.14 • 1 Singapore Dollar = $1.09

Usual prices

Dorm bed: $20-$35 • Budget private room: $50-$80 • Budget eat-in meal: $8-$10 • Supermarket ready-made meal: $3-5 • Bottled drink: $2.50-$4 • Local bus ticket: $2-$3

Average daily costs for budget travelers

Note that costs will be much lower if you use free accommodation and/or don't pay for transportation, but here are some averages to help you get an idea of how much you'll need: Single Traveler: $30-$50 • Multiple travelers: $25-$40 per person

Money

In New Zealand the card is king, so if you have a card that does not charge a fee to use abroad, or you are able to get a card here if on a working holiday visa, definitely try to use the plastic to save on cash withdrawal fees. Cards are pretty much accepted anywhere, so you'll only need cash for emergencies. If you don't have access to such a card, make sure you regularly check www.supercheapguides.com to keep an eye on the exchange rates. When taking out money, you'll usually get better rates by using an ATM than going to a counter, so check your bank withdrawal fees and get out a large amount each time to cut down on fees. Tipping is done at fancy restaurants, but is not generally customary here.

Electricity

New Zealand has an electricity supply that runs at 230V AC (50Hz), with two or three angled pin plugs. These are the same as in Australia or some other parts of Asia. If coming from elsewhere, make sure you pick up an adapter before coming here.

Visas

New Zealand allows visa free travel from most countries for tourists, but make sure you check with your local New Zealand embassy. If you are interested in working for accommodation, consider getting a working holiday visa if they are available for your nationality.

Travel SIM cards

Tourists in New Zealand should also consider getting a data SIM card if they don't want any hassle with crappy wifi. Spark and Vodafone have branches at most airports where you can pick these up, but low-cost carrier Skinny is also worth considering. Note that in rural areas there may not be any reception, and that as the former national provider, Spark has the best coverage. Another plus for Spark customers is that they get access to more than 1000 wifi spots across the country.

Best free apps to download before you go

- Bookme.co.nz is the go-to website and app for discount tours and activities in New Zealand. Always check prices on this before booking anything in New Zealand.
- Skyscanner for comparing cheap airplane tickets.
- Trade Me, New Zealand's version of eBay and Craigslist. Buy used cars, cheap winter sports gear and lots more.
- Booking.com to quickly cancel or amend bookings. Airbnb is also worth downloading.
- Google Maps or Maps.me, then download the areas you will be visiting.
- XE Currency for comparing prices to back home.
- Splittr, which allows you to see who owes what to who when traveling with friends.
- CamperMate shows the locations of public toilets, garbage bins, campsites, free wifi and a lot more across New Zealand.
- Star Chart is a must download if you are interested in stargazing under New Zealand's clear skies. Using AR it tells you which stars you're looking at in real time on the screen.
- The Department of Conservation has a campsite finder app, as well as a very useful website for those that want to find campsites or plan a hike.
- The Met Service app and website are useful for checking tide levels and the weather.

Auckland

New Zealand's largest city, Auckland is a beautiful mix of nature and urban life. The city where most people start their adventures, it has a sunny climate, an unexpected diversity of food for a city of its size and a rich history of Polynesian culture. In a city where most people are within an hour of a beach, it's certainly more chilled out and relaxed than most big cities. With so many things to do and lots nearby, Auckland really hits the spot for budget travelers.

Getting around

Most of the sights are a leisurely walk from the city center or a short bus ride away. The city has an extensive and easy-to-use transportation network, with buses, ferries and trains. The two bus routes that most tourists will use are the InnerLink (green buses) and the OuterLink (oranges buses), which connect all the major attractions to the city center. The $1 CityLink bus is also useful if you need to move heavy luggage along Queen Street, the main road in the city center.

You can pay with cash, but if you're going to be here for a few days or more it might be worth getting an AT Hop electronic card. With this card, buses are around 30% cheaper compared to paying with cash, so if you think you'll save more than the $10 deposit it's a worthwhile purchase. Visitors can also load a day pass on to their AT Hop card for $18.

Things to do

Auckland Art Gallery / Toi o Tamaki

This recently built gallery has a captivating selection of ever-changing exhibitions. Both modern art and art going back hundreds of years is on display. Check the website before going to see what's on, or just pop in when you have a free hour or so. *FREE • 10am-5pm •* www.aucklandartgallery.com

Auckland War Memorial Museum

While not as impressive or as new as the Te Papa in Wellington, this museum has a huge display of everything related to Auckland. The focus of much of it is war, and war veterans, of course, with moving halls listing the names of those who have fallen and exhibitions on the various wars that New Zealand has participated in during its short existence. On the lower levels there are some excellent exhibitions about New Zealand's nature and Maori people, such as a re-creation of a traditional Maori hut. Also has a play area for children, with a host of educational activities. *FREE for locals (bring proof, or just say your address in Auckland at the ticket office), otherwise adults $25, children $10 • 10am-5pm •* www.aucklandmuseum.com *• Take the green InnerLink bus from Queen Street (10 mins, adults $3.50, children $2)*

Sky Tower

Climb 328 meters up Auckland's tallest building for a 360-degree view of the city and nearby islands. It's not an essential visit for the price, but many people want to tick off this iconic tower. *Adults $32, children $13, under six years old FREE (see the website for available discounts) • 9am-9:30pm •* www.skycityauckland.co.nz *• Up Victoria Street West, a few minutes on foot from the center*

Mount Eden Summit

A much better way to get a view over the city, because it's free, is to walk up to the summit of this dormant volcano. At the top is a 50-meter deep crater from the last eruption more than 15,000 years ago and uninterrupted views of the city. *Difficulty: Easy • Time required: 1-2 hours return • By bus: the easiest way is to take the OuterLink bus (15 mins, adults $3.50, children $2) from the city center to Mount Eden, then walk from there. By car: it's about 10 minutes south from the center. Parking is available at the bottom of the mountain*

Walk along the waterfront

Take a free stroll down the waterfront, grab an ice cream or some fish and chips along the way and enjoy the cool, breezy air and view across the harbor. At the end is the Silo Park, which often has little events or festivals on, especially in the summer.

Downtown Auckland

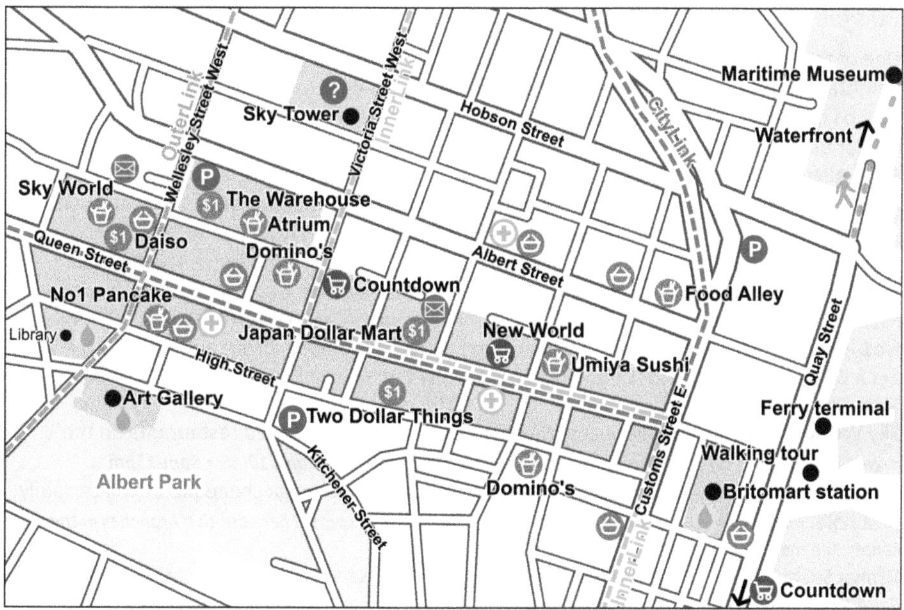

New Zealand Maritime Museum

Built to celebrate the vital role that sailing has played in New Zealand's history, from the courageous Polynesian people who came here thousands of years ago to British explorers such as James Cook. A highlight is a recreation of an old convenience store, called a 'dairy' in New Zealand, stacked with retro food packaging and old-fashioned architecture. Suitable for all ages, but very much skippable if you're left satisfied after visiting the other museums. *FREE for locals (bring proof), otherwise adults $20, children $10, family passes $40 • 10am-5pm •* www.maritimemuseum.co.nz *• Located on the waterfront*

Auckland Zoo

Home to the largest collection of animals in the country, Auckland Zoo has more than 1,400 animals and a hundred species. It does a great job of showing off the diversity of the wildlife in New Zealand. Fun events and animal encounters spice up the experience too, and are great fun for the little ones. *FREE • 9:30am-5pm •* www.aucklandzoo.co.nz *• By bus: from downtown, buses 18 and 133 go to the zoo (15 mins, adults $5.50, children $3). Get off at bus stop 8124 on Great North Road. By car: the zoo is on Motions Road, 15 minutes west of downtown Auckland. Free parking provided*

Discount stores

The best prices can usually be found at Japan Dollar Mart, on the basement level next to the Specsavers opticians on Queen Street (10am-7pm). Up the road is Daiso, which packs a lot of cheap Japanese items into its small store (9:30am-10pm). Another good bet is Two Dollar Things on High Street (10am-10pm) and The Warehouse on Elliot Street (8am-8pm), which also sells dirt cheap clothes and electronics.

Free guides and tours

Free daily guided walks are available with Auckland Free Walking Tours (www.afwt.co.nz). Leaving from Queens Wharf Village (just outside the downtown ferry terminal) at 10am, the three-hour tours take you around some of the city center highlights, with friendly and generally informative commentary from the enthusiastic guides. Bookings are not essential.

Budget food

One of the best things about Auckland is that a few hawker markets still exist, offering cheap, non-brand takeout and dining options. Outside of these, while there are lots of places that may be comparatively expensive for most tourists, there are a few interesting places to check out for budget travelers:

Food Alley - Excellent prices, and large portions at most of the outlets, can be found here. Food Alley excels in Asian food, with family-run joints selling Thai, Malaysian, Singaporean, Japanese and Chinese cuisine. *Meals $10-14 • 10:30am-9pm • Next to NZ Gifts on Albert Street*

Atrium on Elliott - Another tasty spot to try international food on a budget, this hawker market has several options for all kinds of tastes. *Meals $8-16 • 9am-6pm (5pm on weekends) • Head down to the basement level of the Atrium on Elliott shopping mall, where The Warehouse is located*

No1 Pancake - This Korean pancake joint is rather famous among locals, and a nice place to get a light meal or snack to keep you going. *Pancakes $4-6 • 10:30am-5:30pm (until 4:30pm on Saturdays, closed Sundays)*

Sky World - This entertainment complex has lots of reasonably priced restaurants on the lower floor, again with decent portion sizes and few chains. *Meals $10-16 • 9am-11pm*

Domino's - Popular with backpackers on tight budgets, these mega cheap pizzas will certainly fill a hole. *Pizzas from $5 (order online for best prices) • 10am-11pm • There are two branches in the city center, see map for locations*

Umiya Sushi - Some of the cheapest sushi in town. *Sushi $1-5 • 9:30am-6pm (until 5pm on Saturdays, closed Sundays)*

Cheap supermarkets

There is a small New World supermarket on Queen Street (7am-10pm), but much larger is Countdown on Victoria Street West (7am-10pm). If you are driving and want to pick up some supplies, head to the even bigger Countdown on the east side at 76 Quay Street (24h).

Recommended cheap accommodation

Haka Lodge

Situated on the increasingly trendy Karangahape Road, Haka Lodge is well known as a hostel that delivers a comfy bed and friendly atmosphere. It's sometimes more expensive than other hostels, but here you really get what you pay for, with much better quality rooms than most. *Beds from $28 • 373 Karangahape Road, Auckland, 1010 • Tel: 09 379 4559•* www.hakalodge.com

YHA Auckland City

Once you've checked in, you'll soon see the positive effects of a recent $3 million refurbishment. A great kitchen and very well-equipped rooms. Note that YHA have another branch down the road, while BBH have several across Auckland. *Beds from $23 (10% off for YHA members) • 18 Liverpool Street, Auckland Central • Tel: 09 309 2802 •* www.yha.co.nz

---

How to get there and away

By bus

InterCity, the main national bus operator, has many routes coming out from Auckland, such as to Rotorua (4 hours, $22-$32), Taupo (5 hours, $27-$40) and Wellington (11 hours, $31-$50), including overnight buses to save on accommodation costs. It's also a good place to start your bus passes with Kiwi Experience or Stray.

By car or campervan

Auckland is nearly two hours north of Hamilton via State Highway 1. Rotorua is three hours away down State Highway 27.

By air

All the major airlines such as Air New Zealand, Qantas, Singapore Airlines and Virgin Australia fly here. Budget airline Jetstar has a hub in Auckland too, and flies from many destinations across New Zealand and internationally to Australia, with connections to most major cities in Asia. Coming from Europe, flying via one of the Middle Eastern airlines such as Qatar Airways or Emirates should be considered to keep costs down. Always check websites such as Skyscanner and be as flexible with dates as you can to save to the max!

Getting to and from the airport, the easiest option is to take the SkyBus, which takes you straight into the city and operates 24 hours (40 mins, $18). A cheaper but slower option is to take the 380 Airporter bus service to Papatoetoe train station, then take the train to Britomart, Auckland's main train station (around 1 hour, adults $7.50, children $4).

Free Wifi

The free wifi set up on the waterfront and Queen Street is rather unreliable at times. Better is the Central City Library or the tourist information center. Britomart station also has a good connection most of the time. Arriving at Auckland Airport, the free wifi is excellent.

Tourist information

The Auckland i-SITE Visitor Information Centre is in the Sky Tower building (9am-6pm).

Islands near Auckland

Waiheke Island

Order a glass of wine and relax on Waiheke Island

Just like the British go to Majorca and the Americans go to Hawaii, Aucklanders get away from it all on Waiheke Island. The pristine landscape, even more laidback way of life and copious wineries are a perfect escape from the concrete of downtown Auckland. There are beaches to relax on and do a spot of swimming, lots of island walking trails to venture out into and plenty of ways for budget travelers to keep costs down.

Getting around

A decent bus network connects up the main spots on the west of the island, which contains most places you'll want to visit. The buses are frequent enough and also timed to meet up with ferry departures and arrivals. Fuller, the ferry company that takes visitors to the island, sells day passes for the buses on the island (adults $12, children $6), which are worth getting if you want to do a lot in a day trip. Some buses also have bike racks on the front.

Things to do

Beaches

Oneroa Beach
The most accessible beach on the island, so come here if you only have a day to spare. Head over to the eastern side of the beach for the best views. Near Oneroa Village, the main settlement here. *30 minutes from the wharf or short walk from Oneroa Village (bus routes A, B, F or G)*

The almost never crowded Onetangi Beach

Onetangi Beach

By far the longest beach on Waiheke Island, Onetangi has some of the whitest sand, plus free public gas BBQs and picnic tables. There's always lots of space, whatever time of the year, plus Onetangi Beach is often a perfect spot for a swim or surf. *Take bus route A or F all the way to Onetangi Beach*

Palm Beach

A favorite spot for families and kids wanting to do a bit of sandcastle building, Palm Beach has good facilities such as public BBQs, plus a children's playground. It's known to have calmer tides than many other beaches on the island, so is a good bet for a swim. *Take bus route B to Palm Beach*

Island walks

There are several walks and hikes that can be done around the island, but here are some of the best for day-trippers and those using the buses:

Onetangi Reserve

Also known as the Forest & Bird Reserve, a myriad of walking and hiking trails wind their way through this forest wilderness. It's also recommended by locals for bird watching, such as for the kaka parrot. *Difficulty: Easy to medium • Time required: Various hikes ranging from 10 minutes to a few hours • Located behind Onetangi Beach, accessible via Waiheke Road or bus route E*

Church Bay Circuit

Why not get a bit of exercise first, then reward yourself with wine at the end, or on the way if you're feeling naughty? The Church Bay Circuit is a loop course that starts from the southern end of Matiatia Bay, where the ferries arrive. From here you'll go up to a lookout for views over the bay, then follow a coastal trail around Te Miro Bay and Church Bay. Finally you can either turn back on yourself or head down the road to Oneroa Village. *Difficulty: Medium • Time required: 3 hours return • Trail starts from near the wharf (Matiatia Bay)*

Matiatia to Oneroa Beach

See some stunning coastal views north from the wharf. Head up to peaceful Cable Bay, then around to Owhanake Bay. Follow the markers to Korora Road, or head around Island Bay if that track is open. You'll eventually end up at Oneroa Beach, so this route is a perfect way to save on the cost of the bus if you want to go here. Note that there are occasional track closures, so check at one of the ferry terminals or an information center before. *Difficulty: Medium • Time required: 3-4 hours • Starts from the ferry terminal and wharf at Matiatia*

Wineries

The wineries on the island are quite expensive, so budget travelers should just try one, or two if they are real wine fans. It's also best to skip the expensive wine tours unless you are super keen to learn about the history and process of making the stuff. There are more than a dozen on the island, but here are a few highlights:

Stonyridge Vineyards

A very cozy, comfortable place to have a glass, with leather sofas and simple, rustic architecture. There are a number of wineries around this area, such as Te Motu Vineyard and Wild on Waiheke, so it's recommended to explore the area a bit on foot. *Wine tasting from $15 • 10:30am-5pm (6pm on Saturdays and Sundays) •* www.stonyridge.com *• Take the bus to 82 Onetangi Road (bus stop 1114) on routes A, E or F. It's a short walk from there*

Mudbrick Vineyard & Restaurant

The views are stunning from the garden terrace high up on the hill, looking down on the vines and harbor. The cheese boards and other nibbles are also delicious. *Wine tasting from $10 • 10am-5:30pm •* www.mudbrick.co.nz *• It's a 30-40 minute walk from the wharf (Matiatia) or the central town of Oneroa via road. Alternatively, you can walk here via the coastal track in 1-2 hours*

Budget food

Bringing over a picnic or food to use on the public BBQs is the best option here, but there is also a Four Square supermarket in Oneroa Village (7:30am-8:30pm). Eating at most of the wineries can really hurt your bank balance, so best to eat out at takeaway joints such as these:

The Local - Hoki (white fish), Kumara fries and more deep-fried treats. *Meals $10-15 • 11am-3pm, 5pm-8pm (closed Wednesdays, open on evenings Thursday to Saturday) • Next to Four Square in Oneroa Village*

Too Fat Buns - Awesome burger joint. *Burgers from $8 • 12pm-8:30pm Fridays to Sundays, 4pm-8:30pm Wednesdays and Thursdays (closed Mondays and Tuesdays) • Opposite Four Square*

I Love Crepes - Perfect for a light meal or dessert, this creperie is a popular spot. *Crepes from $8 • 11am-6pm (until 7pm Saturdays and Sundays, closed Mondays) • Few shops down from Too Fat Buns*

Recommended cheap accommodation

Waiheke Backpackers Hostel

Rooms to suit solo travelers as well as families and groups are available at this reputable hostel. Amazing view of the beach and a BBQ on the outside terrace. *Private rooms from $85, dorms from $33 • Tel: 09 372 7003 • 421 Seaview Road, Onetangi •* www.aucklandcouncil.govt.nz

Bioshelter Backpackers

Very eco-friendly budget accommodation, with large communal eating and sleeping areas. A great place to meet fellow travelers. *Private rooms from $70, dorms $30 (multi-day discounts available) •* bioshelter@hotmail.com *• 33 Pacific Parade, Waiheke Island •* www.facebook.com/BioshelterBackpackers

---

How to get there and away

There are frequent departures from Auckland's downtown ferry terminal with Fullers (40 mins, adults $40, children $20 for day return tickets). AT Hop card fares equate to the same cost and can be used on different days, so are worth using if staying on the island.

Tourist information

Fullers have a little office at the downtown ferry terminal area (8am-6pm).

Rangitoto Island

You'll see this island in the distance as you walk along the Auckland waterfront, with its iconic cone shape something no one can miss. Formed more than 600 years ago, it erupted unexpectedly from the sea and is now the largest volcano in the Auckland region. Bring your lunch with you, as there are no shops on the island.

Things to do

Hike to the summit

This hike sees visitors going in and out of the lava fields and native forest, before making their way up to the summit for a spectacular view of Auckland and the Hauraki Gulf. Along the way there are interesting displays about all the volcanic activity and the history of those that actually lived on Rangitoto. It's the busiest walk on the island, so try to get the earliest ferry to beat the crowds. *Difficulty: Easy • Time required: 2-3 hours return • Follow signs from Rangitoto Wharf*

Lava caves

A worthwhile detour when doing the summit walk, hikers are able to walk through the caves left behind from the passage of lava after the big eruption. You'll need to use your phone's torch function down here, as it gets very dark. *Difficulty: Easy • Time required: Extra 20-30 minutes • Located near the summit, follow signs on the eastern side as you go up the summit track*

Coastal track

Winding past old boats, war ruins and volcanic remains, this track is usually pretty empty of people. It's also an excellent addition if you think you're fast enough to get the ferry back in time, and can be combined with the summit track to make a circular route around the island. *Difficulty: Easy • Time required: 2-3 hours • Head east from Rangitoto Wharf*

How to get there and away

Fullers have a ferry service from the downtown ferry terminal to Rangitoto Wharf, with a few services in the morning to the island, then a few back in the afternoon (adults $36, children $18, families $97). Cheaper early bird tickets are available on weekends and public holidays when taking the 7:30am ferry. Check www.fullers.co.nz at least the day before.

Auckland to Wellington

Rotorua

Wai-O-Tapu in Rotorua is quite a sight when you see it with your own eyes

Rotorua is New Zealand's hot spring capital. The town and surrounding area are dotted with explosive geysers, hot bubbling mud pools and clouds of steam. This geothermal theme park is a real marvel, and there are plenty of ways to enjoy it, such as forest walks, soaking yourself in a hot spring bath, or just walking around the town with your camera!

Things to do

Tourist spots in central Rotorua

Kuirau Park
Take a stroll in this large public park and you'll get to see plenty of bubbling and steaming geothermal activity. Eruptions are very rare, but they do very occasionally occur, such as in 2001 when mud and rocks the size of footballs shot out more than 10 meters high, so be careful and stay in the safe areas! *FREE • 24h*

Sulphur Point
Another exciting place to take a walk or bike to if you are interested in checking out Rotorua's geothermal activity. Continue around the boardwalk and you'll get a beautiful view of more boiling mud pools and streaming vents, as well as across the bay. *Difficulty: Easy • Time required: 1-2 hours on foot, 30-40 minutes by bicycle*

Government Gardens
Historic English garden with a Tudor-style bath house and some very ornate pieces of architecture. The area was the site of many significant battles between Maori and was given to the crown in the 1800s. The government then cleared the area and created this posh garden using Japanese firs and Californian weeping redwood. Worth visiting on the way to Sulphur Point, or if you have a bit of time to spare. *FREE • 8am-8pm*

Te Papaiouru Marae and the Ohinemutu area

Head here rather than going to the expensive Maori 'village experience' in the Government Gardens. Ohinemutu used to be a Maori village, and still has the 'Te Papaiouru Marae', a Maori meeting house, and St Faith's Anglican Church, a traditional building that's also worth checking out. *Head north past Ali Baba's and Lady Jane's Ice Cream Parlour, then continue up to the Anglican church, via the meeting house. It takes about 10-15 minutes on foot*

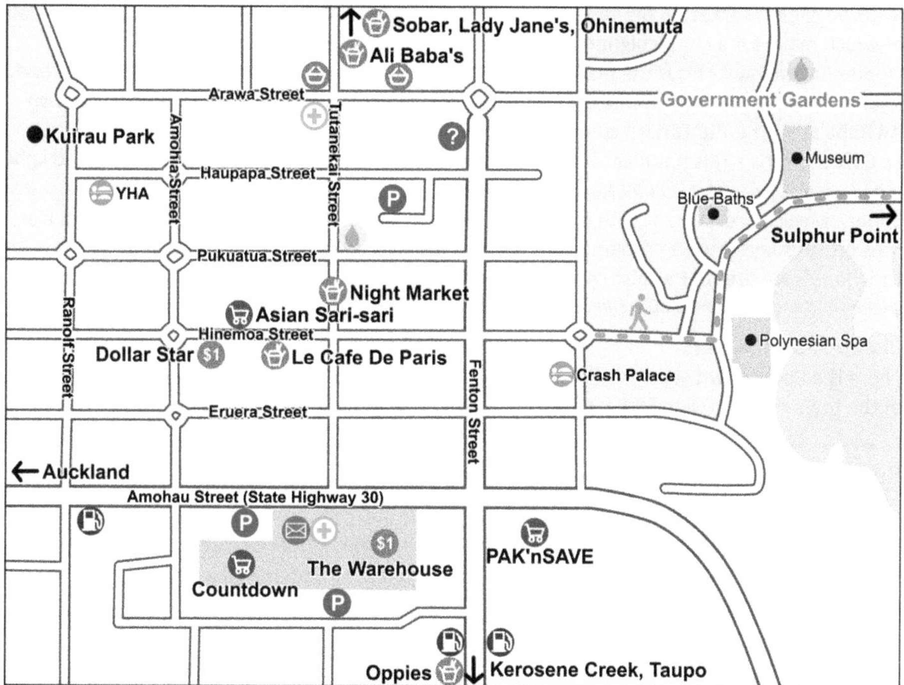

Geothermal experiences outside town

Kerosene Creek

Stunningly picturesque thermal pool and waterfall. It's possible for visitors to bathe in the hot water too, as little baths have been created using nearby rocks. It's a lovely experience, if it's not too busy, surrounded by lush native forest. *FREE • 24h • Just over 30 minutes by car south of Rotorua, via State Highway 5*

Wai-O-Tapu Thermal Park

Probably the most impressive area of geothermal activity near Rotorua, Wai-O-Tapu Thermal Park is the place to see the steaming orange pools known as the 'Champagne Pools'. There are about a dozen of these in the area, all linked by walking tracks and hill roads. Another highlight is the Lady Knox Geyser, which is induced to jet off water every day just after 10am, reaching heights of up to 20 meters. As you explore the area, you'll come across a few spots to soak your body in too, such as a fun mud pool and a free hot pool under the road bridge just outside the park. *Difficulty: Easy • Time required: around 2-3 hours to see it all • Adults $32.50, children $11 • 8:30am-5pm •* www.waiotapu.co.nz *• By bus: InterCity has a few coaches every day that stop nearby from Rotorua (30 mins, $10). Headfirst Travel (*http://headfirsttravel.com*) has tours that include Waiotapu (adults from $85, children from $51). Thermal Shuttle (*https://thermalshuttle.co.nz*) also provides transport-only options (from $65). By car: about 35 minutes by car south of Rotorua, via State Highway 5, past Kerosene Creek • By bicycle: it's possible to cycle back after using Thermal Shuttle to get there, or you could do a return trip to save money. Kerosene Creek could also be done on the way back*

Discount stores

The Warehouse has a large store to the south of the town center (8am-9pm). The smaller Dollar Star also has a reasonably good range (9am-5pm).

Budget food

Rotorua Night Market - A big variety of locally-owned food stalls and trucks, plus live music, all of which make for a cheap night out. *Meals $10-$15 • 5pm-9pm every Tuesday*
Oppies Takeaway - This is the place to get yourself some cheap fish and chips or Chinese food. It has won plenty of awards and is loved by the locals. *Snacks from $3, meals $6-10 • 11am-10pm*
Ali Baba's - Authentic Turkish cuisine. *Meals $10-16 • 11:30am-9pm (closed Sundays)*
Le Cafe De Paris - This popular cafe has all sorts of tasty French breads, salads, crepes and light meals. *Breads from $4, meals $9-$14 • 10am-4pm (closed Sundays and Mondays)*
Sobar - Mexican restaurant with plenty of deals throughout the week, such as $9 nachos, free fries on Tuesdays and $1 chicken wings on Wednesdays. *Meals from $9-15 • 11am-1am*
Lady Jane's Ice Cream Parlour - An iconic ice cream shop that's been going for decades. *Ice creams and snacks from $3.50 • 10am-9pm (until 6pm Sundays to Wednesdays)*

Cheap supermarkets

There is a Countdown supermarket (7am-10pm) and a PAK'nSAVE (7:30am-10pm) to the south of the town center. Asian Sari-sari also has some excellent special offers (10am-6pm).

Recommended cheap accommodation

Crash Palace

This lively hostel has frequent events, and provides complimentary tea, coffee, rice, pasta, herbs and oils, so you'll save a bit if you self-cater while staying here. *Private rooms from $50, dorms from $17 • Tel: 07 348 8842 • 1271 Hinemaru Street, Rotorua •* www.crashpalace.co.nz

YHA Rotorua

Really well-regarded hostel located in a modern building with great facilities. *Beds from $25 (10% off for YHA members) • Tel: 07 349 4088 • 1278 Haupapa Street, Rotorua •* www.yha.co.nz

Rotorua Central Backpackers (BBH)

Friendly hostel with comfy single beds and unlimited free wifi. *Beds from $28 (from $24 with BBH card) • Tel: 07 349-3285 • 1076 Pukuatua Street, Rotorua •* www.rotoruacentralbackpackers.co.nz

How to get there and away

By bus

InterCity have lots of buses heading to Rotorua, for example from Auckland (4 hours, $25) and Taupo (1 hour, $12). Kiwi Experience and Stray both go via Rotorua on many of their routes.

By car or campervan

Rotorua is about three hours from Auckland, one hour from Taupo and just under one hour from Hobbiton. There are many gas stations in the town.

By air

Few budget travelers come to Rotorua by air, as the buses are so much cheaper. Air New Zealand fly here from the main cities. Cityride Rotorua provides buses into the town ($2.30).

Tourist information

The Rotorua i-SITE is conveniently located in the town center (7:30am-6pm).

Hot Water Beach

Have a great deal of fun digging your own hot water pool in the sand at this rather unusual beach. The naturally heated thermal mineral water from under the sand will then fill up the holes that you dig. It's a really relaxing, and somewhat odd, way to spend an afternoon! If you can, bring your own spade, but you can also hire them from one of the nearby cafes or use something as a make-shift shovel.

You'll need to dig your little spa at low tide, so that the tide is low enough for the area of sand with hot water underneath to be exposed. Two hours either side of low tide is usually best, just note that as lots of people will flock there at this time, it can get mighty busy. To find out when is best on the day, head to www.thecoromandel.com/weather-and-tides or use the Met Service.

Budget food

There are a few cafes on the Pye Place near the beach. Hot Waves Cafe have a wide range of salads, pasta and burgers for $14-$18 (8:30am-4pm), while down the road Hotties Beachfront Eatery offers similar fare, but with sea view (10am-4pm). With these slightly high prices though, it might be better to eat before or bring food with you.

Recommended cheap accommodation

Hot Water Beach TOP 10 Holiday Park

Well-run complex on the main road near the beach. All sorts of private cabins and units, a backpacker hostel and plenty of sites for tents and campervans. *From $20 • Tel: 07 866 3116 • 790 Hot Water Beach Road, RD1 Whitianga •* www.hotwaterbeachtop10.co.nz

Auntie Dawns Place

Two comfy self-contained units, with complimentary tea, coffee, bread and cereal for your breakfasts included. There is also a space outside for campers. *Camping spaces from $20, private units from $100 • Tel: 07 866 3707 • Auntie Dawns Place, 15 Radar Road •* www.auntiedawn.co.nz

How to get there and away

By bus

Stray and Kiwi Experience go here on some of their North Island and national passes, but not all of them. At the time of going to press, InterCity do not have a service to Hot Water Beach.

By car or campervan

Hot Water Beach is about two hours from Auckland, via State Highways 1 and 25. It's almost three hours down to Rotorua. There are three car parks near the beach, with just the Main Beach car park charging a fee, while the others are usually free.

Waitomo Glowworm Caves

A maze of caves and underground rivers can be found below the green hills of Waitomo, making for a cool little detour as you head from Auckland to Wellington. The easiest way to see the caves and the glowworm inhabitants is to join a boat tour. These famous tours come with a guide, who will provide expert commentary about the environment and the cave's history. While prices may seem high, there are various discounts available, such as a 'Kids go FREE' offer and other seasonal deals. There are also walking tours, but budget travelers should consider the Ruakuri Walk, a free self-guided loop track that starts from the Waitomo Adventures car park (or you can walk from Waitomo town via the Waitomo Walkway). Taking about one hour, this spectacular course takes walkers through forested gorges, past limestone bluffs and through dark caves adorned with stalactites and stalagmites. If you go at night you may see glowworms for the grand price of $0! *Boat tours: adults $53, children $24 • Tours depart every half hour from 9am-5am •* www.waitomo.com *• By bus: InterCity has a direct service from Auckland (3 hours, $100) and Rotorua (2 hours, $40). Kiwi Experience and Stray also go to Waitomo. By car: Waitomo is just over two hours from Auckland via State Highway 1, or two hours from Rotorua*

Hobbiton

Take a guided tour into Middle-earth, and visit the original Hobbiton movie set from The Lord of the Rings trilogy and The Hobbit movies. It is situated in a large sheep farm, and visitors will get to see fan favorites like Bags End, where Frodo and Bilbo began their adventure, and the Green Dragon Inn, where you'll be able to grab a beer of your own. Along the way the experienced guides provide a detailed insight into how the sets were made, as well as the story of how the movies came about. It may not be the cheapest thing to do in New Zealand, but if you're a big fan of The Lord of the Rings then it's really a must visit. For others, it's probably best to save your money and spend it elsewhere. *Standard entrance fee: adults $84, children $42, under 9 years old FREE • 9am-3:30pm (additional later tours sometimes operate in summer) •* www.hobbitontours.com *• By bus: InterCity usually have the cheapest tour prices from Rotorua ($113) or Auckland ($159), and can also drop you off in another town or city after. Additionally, Hobbiton Tours have tours with complimentary transportation from the nearby town of Matamata. By car: first make your way towards Matamata, which is two hours from Auckland and one hour from Rotorua, then follow road signs to Hobbiton*

Stop-off point: Hamilton

If you're heading down from Auckland to Tongariro National Park or the Waitomo Glowworm Caves, you'll probably pass Hamilton on State Highway 1. If you continue straight down the highway then you'll pass through the suburb of Frankton, which has cheap takeout joints like Subway, BurgerFuel and McDonald's if you need some food.

If you want to go to a supermarket, head into the city center for the PAK'nSAVE on Mill Street (7am-10pm) or Countdown on Anglesea Street (7am-10pm). The Warehouse is also located on the same road (8am-10pm).

Taupo

The magnificent Huka Falls in Taupo

Situated at the edge of New Zealand's largest lake, Taupo is a great base for an array of activities, from skydiving, to river walks, to jetboating. Lake Taupo is actually a huge volcano, so the surrounding area is also a hotbed for geothermal activity.

Discount tickets and combos

4Play (www.fourplay.co.nz) offer an awesomely cheap extreme activity package. For just $575, visitors can do a bungy jump, a jetboat ride at Huka Falls, a helicopter flight and go skydiving. If you're interested in these activities, then doing them all together will save you a load of money. Also check out www.bookme.co.nz for some heavy discounts on individual activities.

Things to do

Taupo Tandem Skydiving

With possibly the best prices for skydiving in New Zealand, this company offer four heights, with the lowest and cheapest being 9,000 ft, going all the way up to a frightening 18,500 ft! The scenery is pretty amazing of course, free-falling over the grand lake. Various combos and deals are available on the official website. *From $199 • Various departures from 7am-5pm •* www.taupotandemskydiving.com *• Pickups available from town*

Taupo Bungy

Jump off a platform 47 meters high, by yourself or in tandem with a friend, for a real kick of adrenaline! There are various jump style options that the staff can take you through, as well as a less scary cliff swing experience. Combo deals available on their website. *Adults $180, children $130 • Various departures from 11am-3:30pm •* www.taupobungy.co.nz *• Pickups available from town*

Crater of the Moon

Cheaper than the geothermal parks in Rotorua, Crater of the Moon has a bunch of walking routes around its many steamy craters. *Adults $8, children $4, families $20 • 8:30am-6pm (until 5pm in winter) •* www.cratersofthemoon.co.nz *• Drive up Wairakei Drive from the town, then turn into Karapiti Road, which takes about 10 minutes. Try to hitchhike here if you don't have a vehicle*

Huka Falls

More than 200,000 liters of water are said to plummet through Huka Falls every second, one of Taupo's biggest draws. You'll probably hear the noise as you go by the falls, as the river, normally 100 meters wide, narrows to just 15 meters, pushing the water through a hard volcanic canyon. To get there, it's a five minute drive north of Taupo, you can get transport with Hukafalls Jet, or there are infrequent public buses from town (10 mins, $2). Here are the best activities to do at Huka Falls:

Spa Thermal Park to Huka Falls walk

A pleasant walk along the banks of Waikato River. Along the way you can have a free soak at Otumuheke Stream, a natural hot spring. It's also a good option if you don't have a way to get to Huka Falls on the road. *Difficulty: Easy • Time required: 2 hours one-way • Trail starts from the Spa Thermal Park's car park (follow signs to Waikato River), which is a short drive from town or about one hour on foot. Head down Spa Road, then turn left down Country Avenue to get to the car park*

Hukafalls Jet

An exhilarating 30-minute jetboat ride along the stunning Waikato River. Speeds go up to 80km an hour, with 360-degree spins and close-up views of Huka Falls being the hallmarks of this jetboat ride. Check the official website for combo deals and early bird discounts. *Adults from $135, children from $89, family tickets $359 • Various departure time throughout the day • www.hukafallsjet.com • Free shuttle buses available from the town*

Go for a bike ride or walk to Aratiatia Dam

From Huka Falls you can continue up to Aratiatia Dam. It is about a 14km return trip, so most people cycle (rent from your hostel). The ride takes you through bush and farmland, with routes on both sides of the river if you want to mix things up on the return. Once at the dam, you can see out the rapids that occur when the dam is opened, which is usually at 10am, 12pm and 2pm (plus 4pm in summer). *Difficulty: Easy • Time required: 1-2 hours • Starts from Haka Falls*

Central Taupo map

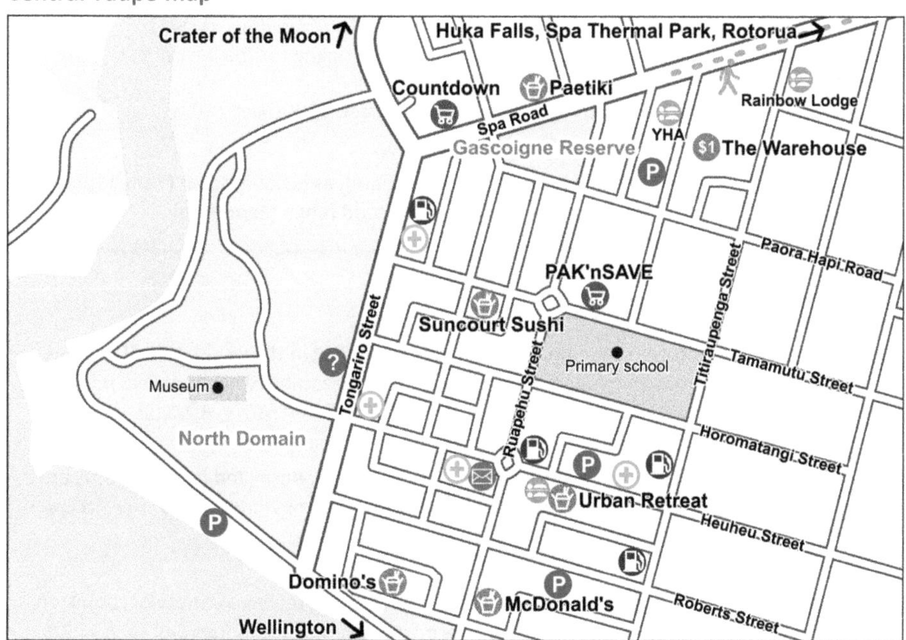

Budget food

McDonald's - When McDonald's opened in Taupo, the land that was bought also included an airplane, so they just decided to turn it into an eating area for the restaurant! It's a rather unusual way to eat one of their cheap burgers, so don't feel ashamed to eat here! *Meals from $3 • 24h*

Taupo Urban Retreat Backpackers - The bar at this hostel is one of the cheapest in town, but the $5 Chilli con Carne is the real winner here. *Meals $5-10 • Chilli con Carne served 6pm-8pm, bar open till late*

Suncourt Sushi - All sorts of colorful, and cheap, sushi. Head here early for a better choice, before things start to sell out. *Sushi boxes from $5 • 8am-4:30pm (closed Sundays)*

Domino's - Cheap pizzas that are sure to fill you up. Order online for the best prices. *Pizzas from $5 • 11am-11pm (until 12am Fridays and Saturdays)*

Paetiki Bakery - Freshly baked pies and tasty pastries. *Snacks $3-5 • 6am-3:30pm*

Cheap supermarkets

Luckily, PAK'nSAVE is very centrally located (7:30am-10pm), as is Countdown (7am-11pm). See the map for locations. The Warehouse also has a good food range (8am-9pm).

Recommended cheap accommodation

Finlay Jack's Backpackers (YHA)

This centrally located hostel, while not in the prettiest building in the world, has all you need for a cheap night's sleep with things like free wifi and a well-equipped kitchen. *Beds from $18 (10% off for YHA members) • Tel: 07 378 9292 • 20 Taniwha Street, Taupo •* www.yha.co.nz

Rainbow Lodge (BBH)

Wifi, tea and the sauna are all free at this funky hostel. Shared, dorm and private rooms are available. *Beds from $26 (from $22 with BBH card) • Tel: 07 378 5754 • 99 Titiraupenga Street, Taupo •* www.rainbowlodge.co.nz

Taupo Urban Retreat

As well as the super cheap bar and food available here, this hostel has a variety of rooms on offer, from family rooms to 16-bed dorms. *Dorms from $15, private rooms from $49 • Tel: 07 378 6124 • 65 Heuheu Street, Taupo •* www.tur.co.nz

How to get there and away

By bus

InterCity have frequent services from Auckland (5 hours, $26), Rotorua (1 hours, $13) and Wellington (6 hours, $27). Both Kiwi Experience and Stray stop off here.

By car or campervan

Taupo is just over three hours from Auckland and five hours from Wellington via State Highway 1, or one hour from Rotorua via State Highway 5.

Tourist information

The i-SITE Visitor Information Centre is located on the west side of town (8:30am-5pm).

Tongariro Alpine Crossing

The most popular day hike on the North Island, the Tongariro Alpine Crossing is a remarkable journey across a vast volcanic landscape. It's a World Heritage area, both for its natural beauty and for its cultural significance, and will surely blow you away with its huge red craters, amazing mountain views, steaming vents and emerald-colored lakes. Make sure you check the weather conditions with the Met Service or at a Department of Conservation office before starting the track. As this is a one-way track, it's best to use a shuttle bus service, back to the start at the end if you have your own vehicle, or from and back to a town like Taupo if you don't have your own vehicle. *Difficulty: Medium • Time required: 7-8 hours one-way • By car: Most people start from the car park down the end of Mangatepopo Road, which is accessed via State Highway 47 to the west. The other end of the track can be accessed via the car park on Ketetahi Road, on State Highway 46 to the north. Note that in summer a four-hour parking restriction is in place at the Mangatepopo car park, so you may need to use a bus. By bus: Adventure HQ (*www.adventurehq.co.nz*) provides return shuttle buses from Taupo ($70). Dempsey Buses (*https://dempseybuses.co.nz*) has buses from National Park Village ($40), Ohakune ($50) and Whakapapa Village ($40). Tongariro Crossing Shuttles (*https://tongarirocrossingshuttles.co.nz*) also has buses from National Park Village ($40)*

Napier

New Zealand's Art Deco capital, Napier has one of the most comprehensive collections of classic 1930s buildings. After a massive 7.8 magnitude earthquake hit the city in 1931, it was quickly rebuilt in this style, and much of it remains to this day. The streets are also lined with palm trees, and the waterfront is full of gardens, memorials and parks, making Napier a lovely place to take a free stroll on a sunny afternoon.

Things to do

Art Deco Centre

It's recommended to make this place your first port of call in Napier. If you're particularly interested in the Art Deco buildings, the center has a $5 short movie called 'The Day that Changed the Bay' that you should watch. *FREE • 9am-5pm*

MTG Hawke's Bay

A museum and art gallery that does a great job of explaining the history of Napier, including the earthquake that destroyed much of the city in 1931 and led to the reconstruction of the city center in its now famous Art Deco style. There are also lots of fine art exhibitions, historical artifacts and traditional Maori objects and items of clothing to view. *FREE • 9:30am-5pm •* www.mtghawkesbay.com

Napier Prison

Head around New Zealand's first prison for a fascinating walkthrough of what life was like for the early prisoners. It's certainly a bit spooky, but it's been made into a super fun experience with things like mugshots and fingerprints to take home as a souvenir. *Adults $20, children $10 • 9am-5pm •* www.napierprison.com *• The prison is located a few minutes up the Marine Parade*

Bluff Hill Lookout

Get a spectacular view over Hawke's Bay and the city center by walking up this nearby hill. Constructed as a gun emplacement, the lookout is usually pretty quiet. *Difficulty: Easy • Time required: 1-2 hours return • Head up Marine Parade. The walk up starts just after passing Napier Prison*

Take a walk around Napier

As well as the Art Deco buildings, the Marine Parade is a pleasant spot to have a walk along, with an amazing beach, sea views and interesting statues along the way. Use the map below for a self-guided tour around some of the Art Deco buildings and the parade:

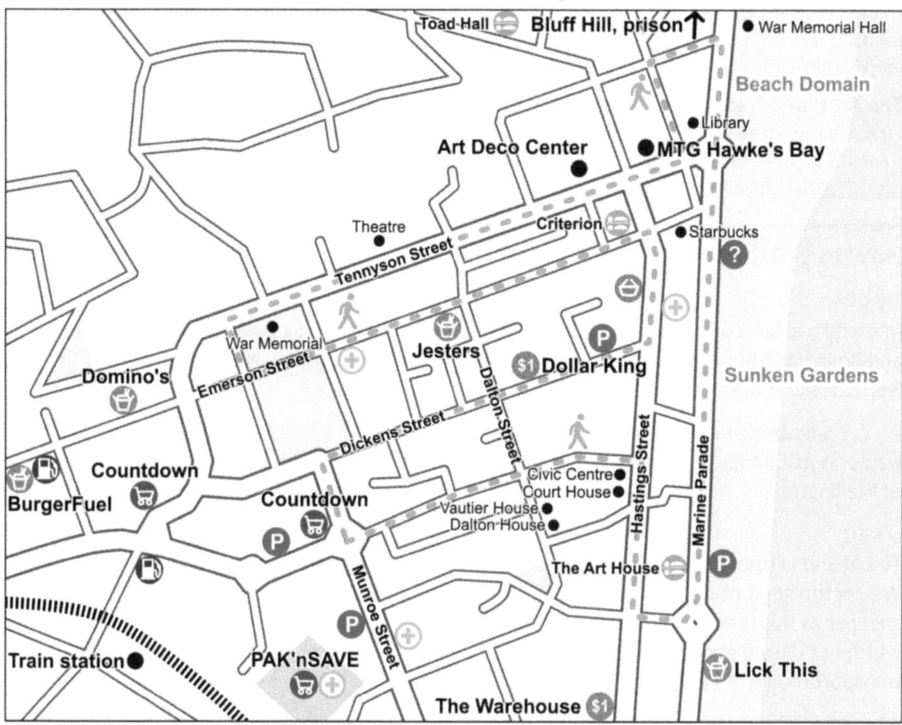

Discount stores

The Warehouse has a decently sized discount store on the south side of Napier (8am-10pm). In the center, Dollar King has everything from cheap toys to stationery (9am-5:30pm).

Budget food

Napier Urban Farmers' Market - Emerson Street hosts this lively market, with some of the best bakers, coffee makers and fruit sellers of the region all coming together in Napier. *Snacks $3-5, takeaway meals from $10 • 9am-1pm every Saturday*

BurgerFuel - New Zealand's most popular gourmet burger chain sells juicy, high-quality burgers with local ingredients. *Meals $8-15 • 10am-10pm*

Jesters - This pie shop has plenty of funny fillings, such as English breakfast and spaghetti bolognaise, and is a good choice for a snack or light meal. *Pies $5-6 • 9am-5pm*

Domino's - Cheap pizzas. Order online for the best prices. *Pizzas from $5 • 11am-12am (Thursday to Saturday), 11am-11pm (Sunday to Wednesday)*

Lick This - More than 43 flavors of ice cream and sorbet, with some delightfully inventive toppings. *Ice creams $2.20-6.50 • 10am-5pm*

Cheap supermarkets

PAK'nSAVE has a big store on the west side of central Napier (7am-10pm). Countdown also has two supermarkets nearby (7am-10pm).

Recommended cheap accommodation

Toad Hall Backpackers
Free breakfast and wifi, plus free soup or dessert on Thursday evenings. There are lots of things to do for free to keep you entertained, such as a pool table and table tennis area. *Dorms from $35, private rooms from $50 • Tel: 06 835 5555 • 11 Shakespeare Road, Bluff Hill •* www.toadhall.co.nz

The Art House Backpackers (BBH)
Ocean views, free wifi and a variety of rooms, all set in a super funky Art Deco building. *Beds from $25 for BBH members, from $29 for non-members • Tel: 06 835-5575 • 259 Marine Parade, Napier •* https://arthousenapier.co.nz

How to get there and away

By bus

Intercity has bus connections to towns such as Taupo (2 hours, $11), Wellington (5 hours, $17) and Rotorua (4 hours, $16). Both Stray and Kiwi Experience drop by Napier on some of their North Island routes.

By car or campervan

Napier is just under two hours from Taupo via State Highway 5, or about four hours north-east of Wellington.

By air

The nearest airport, Hawke's Bay Airport, has flights to major cities such as Auckland, Wellington and Christchurch. If you are already on the North Island, taking a bus is usually cheaper as this is not yet a major airport. The only budget airline that flies here is Jetstar, which has daily flights from Auckland. Super Shuttle (www.supershuttle.co.nz) provides transportation from and to Napier for $20 per person.

Tourist information

The i-SITE Visitor Information Centre is located on the waterfront (9am-5pm). They can also provide more detailed maps about the Art Deco buildings in the area, as well as tours provided by passionate, knowledgeable locals.

Stop-off point: Palmerston North

If you're driving down from Napier or Taupo to Wellington, then you'll probably pass by Palmerston North. It's not really got much to keep you here for long, but it does have lots of essentials like supermarkets and cheap takeaways and restaurants, which can be found in and around the city center, called The Square. Here are some stores that may be of use if heading into the country rather than towards a big town or city:

Kmart - Discount variety store, with a good stock of travel items and clothes. *8am-11pm • Halfway down Fitzherbert Street, south of The Square*

PAK'nSAVE - Big discount supermarket. *8am-10pm • Head down Fitzherbert Street south of The Square and take the first right*

Countdown - Popular supermarket chain. *7am-10pm • Head down Fitzherbert Street south of The Square and take the first right*

Wellington

Wellington's famous cable car

New Zealand's capital city may be a fraction of the size of most, but it's a real powerhouse in culture, cuisine and much more. It's full of art galleries and night markets, plus a grand museum and a lively downtown area. It's also got some excellent hiking spots in the nearby mountains and a harbor in the midst of revitalization, just begging to be explored. Top that off with an old-school cable car, and you've got an enjoyable trip on your hands!

Getting around

The city center is all very walkable, so try to get accommodation that is central, like the ones listed in this chapter. Those that will be using the local bus a lot should get a Snapper card, the local electronic payment card. With this you'll save at least 25% on your journeys compared to using cash and transfers are free. There is a $10 deposit to buy one though, so just get it if you are staying more than a few days and want to go out of the city center many times.

Things to do

The Weta Cave

How could you come to the home of Weta Studios, the geniuses who helped make The Lord of The Rings among other great movies, and not check out their studio? See how they made the models, props and more in the behind-the-scenes tours. Tour staff are very knowledgeable and do lots to make the tours fun for people who aren't familiar with all the movies. *Tours from $28 for adults, $13 for children. Family deals from $72 • 9am-5:30pm •* www.wetaworkshop.com *• Take the 18e bus from Ghuznee Road in the center to stop 6240 on Darlington Road*

Museum of New Zealand / Te Papa Tongarewa

Possibly the most impressive museum in New Zealand, Te Papa, as the locals call it, is the country's national museum. It's a superb introduction to everything that makes this country so fascinating, from the history of the first European settlers and the Maori people, to the amazing creatures that exist here and in the surrounding seas. Don't miss a try on the earthquake simulator! *FREE • 10am-6pm •* www.tepapa.govt.nz

Cable car

Anyone coming to Wellington has to try out the cable car. It's a little clunky and is full of charm, plus it's also a convenient way to get from the city center to the Kelburn Lookout. Once up here, you'll get a spectacular panoramic view of Wellington. One way to save money is to get a one-way ticket, then walk back down into the city via the Botanic Garden. The way down is well signposted. *Adults $5, children $2.50 • 7am-10pm on weekdays, 8:30am-10pm on Saturdays, 8:30am-9pm on Sundays •* www.wellingtoncablecar.co.nz

Cable Car Museum

This interesting little museum illustrates the history of Wellington's iconic cable cars, with a selection of the original vehicles located in the old winding house. *FREE • 8:30am-5pm •* www.museumswellington.org.nz/cable-car-museum *• Located just outside the top cable car station*

Wellington Zoo

One of the best places to see New Zealand's diverse, and at times unexpectedly weird, animal life. From kiwi to rescued blue penguins and foreign animals such as tigers and chimpanzees, there's a whole lot to see and do here for all ages. *Adults $25, children $12, family deals from $49 • 9:30am-5pm • 200 Daniell Street, Newtown, Wellington 6021 •* https://wellingtonzoo.com *• There are reasonably frequent buses to the zoo from the railway station and on Manners Street in the city center*

Wellington Museum

Worth checking out if you're on the waterfront and have a bit of free time on your hands. Full of interesting artifacts and captivating stories about Wellington's history, located in an old heritage building. *FREE • 9am-5pm •* www.museumswellington.org.nz *• Head up the waterfront. The museum is on the other side of the TSB Arena*

Downtown Wellington

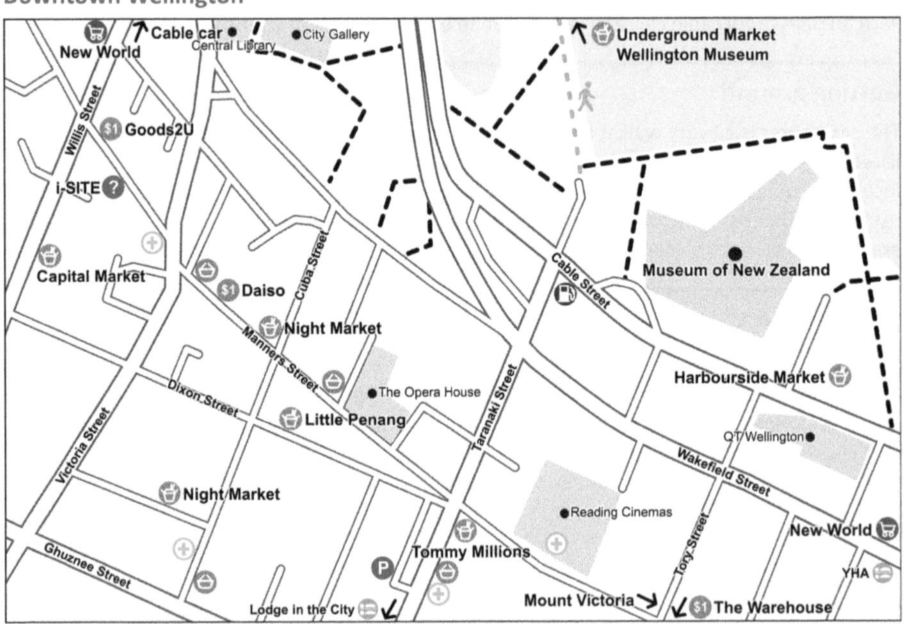

Mount Victoria

Reach the summit of this famous mountain for a world-class 360 degree view of Wellington. Part of the walk was actually used in the filming of The Lord of the Rings, thanks to its breathtaking views. The land has been set aside as a protected area since 1841, left just for walkers and joggers to enjoy. *Difficulty: Easy • Time required: around 1 hour • Head east down Courtenay Place, then continue down Majoribanks Street until you see the sign to the Southern Walkway. Follow the Summit Walkway to the lookout*

Discount stores

Daiso, the Japanese dollar store chain, has a new shop near the i-SITE in the city center (9am-9pm). Nearby, Goods2U has a good selection of cheap souvenirs and travel items (9am-6pm). Megastore The Warehouse has a reasonably central store located just a minute south of where Vivian Street and Tory Street intersect (8am-9pm).

Budget food

Waiting for some cheap fried noodles at the Wellington Night Market

The best places to go in Wellington for cheap food are the markets. All kinds of foods are on display, from Vietnamese noodles to Brazilian BBQ. Expect to pay $8-15 per plate.

Wellington Night Market - This bustling market is a little treasure trove of cheap food stalls, inventive cafes and much more. The Asian and ethnic food on offer is particularly exciting, with Malaysian, Mexican, Indonesian and Sichuan cuisine to dig into. *5pm-11pm on Fridays and Saturdays • Held in Left Bank (off Cuba Street) on Fridays and on lower Cuba Street (near the Manners Street intersection) on Saturdays*

Capital Market - The cheapest market in the city. Down-to-earth grub from local chefs, all with their own little stalls and homegrown brands. *10:30am-9pm • Head up Willis Street, which is near the i-SITE, and make a left turn into the market*

Harbourside Market - All sorts of locally produced fruits, vegetables and condiments, plus some food trucks turning all this fresh produce into tasty takeaways. There is also live music to enjoy. *7:30am-2pm every Sunday • Just across the road from the Museum of New Zealand*

Wellington Underground Market - A vibrant mix of bakers, pizza makers and candy sellers. There is also a strong art component to this market, so you might be able to pick up some souvenirs that can't be bought elsewhere. *10am-4pm every Saturday •* www.undergroundmarket.co.nz *• Head along the waterfront and look out for signs*

Little Penang - Low prices and big portions of authentic Malaysian dishes. One of those places that locals like to head to for lunch. *$14-16 • 11am-3pm, 5pm-9pm*

Tommy Millions - Super cheap pizza slices, as well as Italian hot chocolate and coffees. *Pizza from $5 • 11am-11pm (until 4am Fridays and Saturdays)*

Cheap supermarkets

Minimarts are littered all over the city, but there are some New World supermarkets near the Museum of New Zealand (7am-11pm) and on Willis Street, near the City Gallery (7am-11pm).

Recommended cheap accommodation

YHA Wellington

Huge hostel, with lots of space downstairs to hang out in or just watch a movie. Has any type of room you can imagine, with both ensuite and shared bathrooms. *Beds from $31 (10% off for YHA members) • 292 Wakefield Street, Te Aro, Wellington 6011 • Tel: 04 801 7280 •* www.yha.co.nz

Lodge in the City (BBH)

It's hardly the Hilton, but with these prices how can you complain? *Beds from $16 for BBH members, from $20 for non-members • Tel: 04 385 8560 • 152 Taranaki Street •* www.lodgeinthecity.co.nz

---

How to get there and away

By bus

InterCity have buses and connections from most major towns and cities on the north island, such as Auckland (11 hours, $29-60) and Taupo (6 hours, $27-$42). Both Stray and Kiwi Experience go here.

By car or campervan

Wellington is just over two hours from Palmerston North via State Highway 1 and 57. Further north, Taupo takes about five hours to get to. Park at your accommodation to save money.

By ferry

Both Interislander (from $65) and Bluebridge (from $54) have ferries that go between Wellington and Picton on the South Island in about three and a half hours. Current deals can be found at www.greatjourneysofnz.co.nz/interislander and www.bluebridge.co.nz/deals.

By air

Various airlines, such as budget airline Jetstar, fly to Wellington Airport, but Auckland and Christchurch airports are larger, so entering the country via either of these two is often cheaper, plus there are more choices of route. Singapore Airlines also occasionally have some excellent deals, especially if coming from Europe or Asia. There are frequent local buses into the city, such as the R91 bus (adults $8, children $5) and the express Airport Flyer bus (adults $12, children $9). If you are staying in Wellington for a while get yourself a Snapper card.

Free Wifi

Wellington has a free wifi service in the city center and on the waterfront, but it's quite slow. Alternatively, McDonald's or Starbucks usually have reasonable connection speeds, plus the Museum of New Zealand and Wellington Central Library are also good options.

Tourist information

The i-SITE Visitor Information Centre is located in the center of town (8:30am-9pm).

Wellington to Christchurch

Picton

The town that you'll arrive in if taking the ferry from the North Island, Picton is not just an important transportation hub. It's a rather picturesque spot on the seaside, with a lovely harbor full of trendy cafes, galleries and restaurants. There are also lots of maritime activities on offer here, such as dolphin watching and kayaking.

Things to do

Kaipupu Wildlife Sanctuary

Home to a habitat abundant in unique birdlife and classic New Zealand bush, the Kaipupu Wildlife Sanctuary feels like a world away from the town. Once there, take the two-hour circular walking route, or just the 45-minute return walk to the northern lookout, for the best chance of seeing the birds, as well as hear them sing. The views of the harbor are also rather stunning. *FREE • 24h •* www.kaipupupoint.co.nz *• Short boat ride from Picton waterfront ($20-$30)*

See, and swim with, the dolphins

Head out into the Marlborough Sounds for a chance to view or swim with the local dolphins. The calm waters are a perfect habitat for these majestic creatures, who might on occasion also show off some high leaps, backflips and somersaults for the adoring crowds! Various types of tours are available for different price ranges, so check out local operator E-Ko Tours (www.e-ko.nz) or the i-SITE and the travel agents when you're in town. You could also combine a dolphin tour with a whale tour via E-Ko Tours, which might save you a bit of money and is also worth considering if you're not also going to Kaikoura. *Tours from $99 for adults, $55 for children • A few departures each day, from 8am-6pm • Tours depart from Picton waterfront*

Go kayaking

Rent a kayak and explore the magnificently calm coastline, secluded bays and quiet coves around Picton. Head to the waterfront to rent your kayak, with prices starting from around $40 from operators such as Marlborough Sounds Adventure (www.marlboroughsounds.co.nz).

EcoWorld Picton Aquarium & Wildlife Rehabilitation Centre

The kids will have a whale of a time (pun intended!) here, where they can meet and interact with local animals and marine life. Highlights include the giant squids, seahorses, blue penguins and tuatara, known as 'living fossils'. Feedings are usually at 11am and 2pm every day. *Adults $25, children $12, family passes from $69 • Open from 9:30am (closing time varies day to day)* • www.ecoworldnz.co.nz • *Located at the foreshore, near to the ferry departure point*

The Edwin Fox

Being restored by local history enthusiasts, the Edwin Fox is the ninth oldest ship in the world and the last remaining convict ship. Head inside to learn all about it. *Adults $15, children $5 • 9am-5pm • Short walk north from the tourist information center*

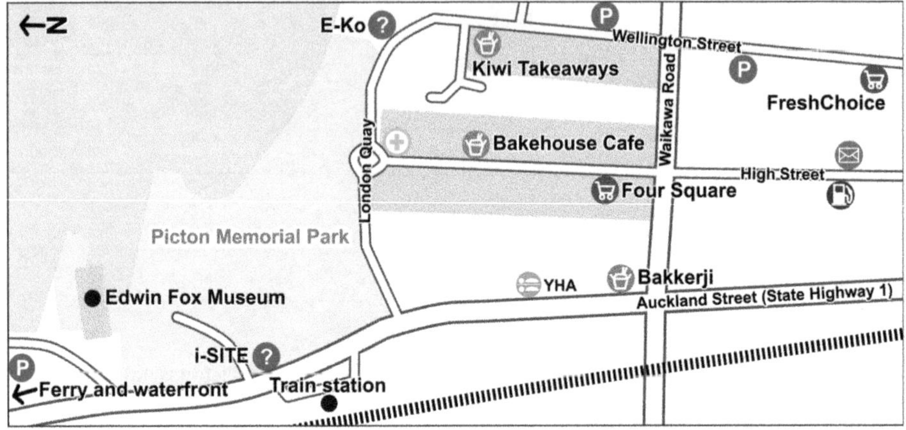

Budget food

Most of the shops, restaurants and takeaways are located south of the information center:
Picton Village Bakkerij - Popular bakery with super tasty pies and fresh sandwiches. *Snacks from $2, light meals $4-10 • 6am-4pm (closed Sundays) • Few minutes south from the station and i-SITE*
Kiwi Takeaways - No-frills fish and chips joint, which also does cheap toasties and burgers. *Fish $3-5, burgers from $6.20 • 11am-2pm, 4:30pm-8pm • On Wellington Street, near the E-Ko Tours office*
Bakehouse Cafe - More sumptuous pies and sandwiches, plus decent breakfasts. *Snacks and pies from $5 • 8am-4pm • Located down High Street, near to the Four Square supermarket*

Cheap supermarkets

A Four Square supermarket is located in the town center (7:30am-9pm), while the larger FreshChoice is a few minutes away on foot, down Wellington Street (7am-7:30pm).

Recommended cheap accommodation

The Villa (YHA)

Charming hostel in a converted boutique character home. Free breakfasts in winter. *Beds from $23 (10% off for YHA members) • Tel: 03 3 573 6598 • 34 Auckland Street, Picton* • www.thevilla.nz

The Jugglers Rest (BBH)

Small hostel, with complimentary bikes to use, plus tea, coffee and eggs in the kitchen, so you can make yourself an omelette and save a bit of money. *Beds from $30 for BBH members, from $34 for non-members • Tel: 03 573 5570 • 8 Canterbury Street, Picton* • www.jugglersrest.com

How to get there and away

By bus

InterCity can take you from Picton towards the west coast, for example to Nelson (2 hours, $28), or down the east coast, such as to Kaikoura (2 hours, $25). Stray and Kiwi Experience both stop at Picton.

By car or campervan

From Kaikoura, you can reach Picton in about two hours via State Highway 1, and the journey from Nelson takes the same time via State Highway 6.

By ferry

You can get to Picton from Wellington via Interislander (from $65) or Bluebridge (from $54) in about three and a half hours. Both occasionally have discounts, so check out www.greatjourneysofnz.co.nz/interislander and www.bluebridge.co.nz/deals.

Tourist information

The i-SITE is across the road from the old station (weekdays 9am-4pm, weekends 10am-3pm).

Kaikoura

Hopefully you'll get lucky and see a display like this!

Kaikoura is New Zealand's premier spot for whale watching, as well as a great place to see dolphins. It's therefore a worthwhile way to break up the journey from Picton to Christchurch if four to five hours on the road seems too long. The marine mammals live permanently in nearby coastal waters, so you'll have a good chance of getting an encounter with them. Whale Watch Kaikoura (www.whalewatch.co.nz) runs a few trips every day from November to March, with a chance to see not just whales, but also dolphins, albatross and fur seals. *Tours from $150 for adults, $60 for children • By bus: InterCity have coaches to Christchurch (3 hours, $18) and Picton (3 hours, $31). Kiwi Experience and Stray also go here. By car: Kaikoura is about halfway between Picton and Christchurch on State Highway 1 and just over two hours from either one*

Christchurch

Outside Canterbury Museum, near the Christchurch Botanic Gardens

Christchurch is the largest city in the South Island and the place most visitors will land in when coming here. In 2010 and 2102 the city was damaged by a series of earthquakes, leading to devastating damage to the city and its people. Since then the people are trying to stay positive, working together to rebuild the city both physically and emotionally. There is still lots of reconstruction going on, particularly in the city center, but this should not hinder your travel experience too much.

Some travelers spend only an afternoon, or a day at most here, while many head straight from the airport to more interesting places such as Lake Tekapo or Arthur's Pass. Having said that though, there are several things you can do in the city to keep you occupied, and many of these are free. The city center is all very walkable, with amazing graffiti and outdoor art dotted all around, so you can enjoy a good stroll in the city before heading off into the countryside and mountains of the South Island.

Things to do

Christchurch Art Gallery

Housed in a grand new building, the city's art gallery has loads of inventive and imaginative exhibitions to visit. There are often special exhibitions, as well as ones especially for kids and families, so definitely check out the official website before going. *FREE • 10am-5pm •* https://christchurchartgallery.org.nz

Canterbury Museum

Worth visiting, especially if you won't be visiting the War Memorial Museum in Auckland. This large museum takes visitors through the history of New Zealand and the Canterbury region, from the formation of the island to the present day. The displays are fun and well presented, with a re-creation of downtown Christchurch in the olden times being a particular highlight. Children can also have fun learning about dinosaurs and about the creepy crawlies that inhabit the region. *FREE • 9am-5pm •* www.canterburymuseum.com

Christchurch Botanic Gardens

The large gardens make for a pleasant stroll if you have a bit of time on your hands. *FREE • 7am-6:30pm*

Bridge of Remembrance

As you're walking around the city, make sure you include this grand bridge. Erected in 1923 to initially honor those lost in the First World War, it now also serves as a memorial to other wars that New Zealanders have fought in.

Christchurch Cathedral

After the earthquakes, Christchurch Cathedral sustained heavy damage. Shut since then, the remaining structures are held up by huge iron rods, scaffolding and shipping containers. Walking around the complex, you can have a look inside and see the current state of the building.

Cardboard Cathedral

Built to replace the cathedral after the earthquakes, this transitional cathedral was designed by renowned Japanese architect Shigeru Ban. He is known for his use of cardboard to create housing for those in disaster areas, and so was tasked with designing this cathedral. The walls, made of eight shipping containers, and the colorful stained glass window help to create a very photogenic piece of architecture.

Cookie Time

Cookie Time is New Zealand's most popular cookie brand, loved across the country. Worth dropping in if you're heading out south, the Cookie Time store has a wide selection of souvenirs based on Cookie Time and its monster mascot, as well as freshly-baked cookies to munch on! *9am-5pm • 789 Main S Road, Templeton, Christchurch 8042 •* https://cookietime.co.nz *• Located on State Highway 1, about 15 minutes by car from central Christchurch*

Downtown Christchurch

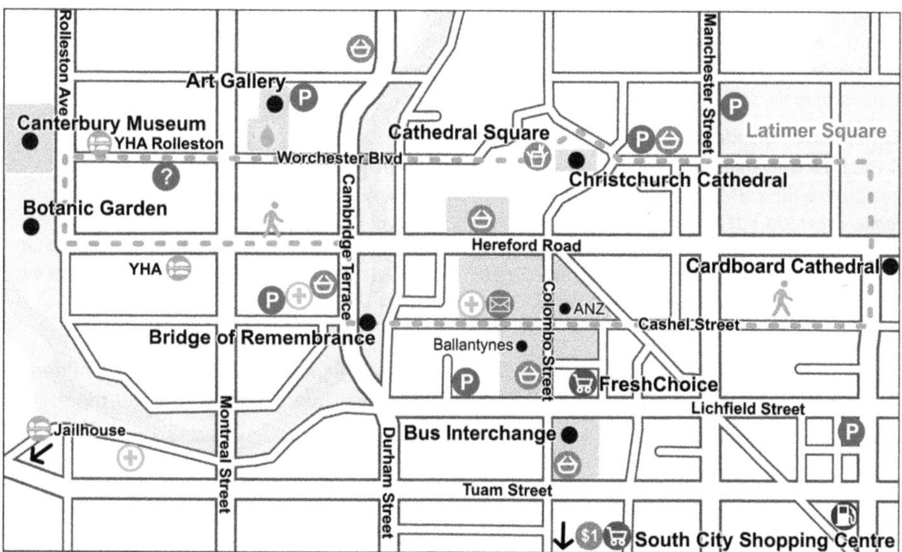

Hikes in Christchurch

Bridle Path

This popular walking track has amazing panoramic views and interesting history panels that really make it worthwhile. It was used by settlers in the area before proper roads had been constructed, and you can imagine how grueling it must have been to transport your goods up this hill. Once at the top (near the gondola's top station), you can either continue down to Lyttelton (catch bus 28 back), return back to the start, or walk along the top of the hill for a bit. *Difficulty: Medium • Time required: 2-3 hours return • Trail starts near the Christchurch Gondola*

Crater Rim Walkway

Joining up with the Bridle Path, it's recommended to head east (passing the gondola if you came up on the Bridle Path) along the Crater Rim Walkway for a bit to escape the crowds and also to see some more spectacular panoramic views. Along the way you'll also see some historic Second World War gun emplacements. *Difficulty: Easy • Time required: 3-4 hours, but you can return to the Gondola when ready • Trail starts from near top gondola station*

Christchurch Gondola

If the idea of walking all the way up seems too much for you, consider taking the famous gondola, which whisks tourists up in about 10 minutes. *Adults $30, children $15, infants FREE, family ticket $75 • 10am-5pm • 10 Bridle Path Road, Heathcote Valley, Christchurch 8022 •* www.christchurchattractions.nz/christchurch_gondola *• By car: about 15 minutes from the city center, in the direction of Lyttelton. By Bus: take route 28 from the bus interchange. There is also a direct shuttle bus, which can be added when you book online (adults $10, children $5).*

Discount stores

The Warehouse has a store in South City Shopping Centre (8am-9pm), full of any kind of item that you'll need for your travels, as well as cheap souvenirs. Take bus route B to get there.

Budget food

As lots of buildings are out of bounds due to the earthquakes, there aren't too many options for eating out on a budget. Quite a few expensive food halls and boutique restaurants have sprung up, but if you're looking for a deal it's best to head to a shopping mall or one of the food trucks that have sprung up across the city, or of course self-cater.

Cathedral Square - Best concentration of food trucks, selling all sorts of foods, from Japanese octopus balls to Greek salads. *Takeout meals $8-12 • Main event 11am-8pm on Fridays, but a smaller number of food trucks and stalls remain on other days • Next to Christchurch Cathedral*

South City Shopping Centre - Mainly chains, but there is also a nice Japanese bakery which is excellent for a light meal, and a few independent takeout joints. *Meal from $10 • 9am-6pm • Take bus route B from the bus interchange if you don't have your own vehicle*

Looking for bargains at Cathedral Square

Cheap supermarkets

There is a FreshChoice in the city center, which has a good selection of breads, meats and fillings if you want to make yourself a sandwich or such (7am-9pm). A better choice if you have your own mode of transportation or don't mind a short bus ride is to head to supermarket chain New World (7am-10pm) in the South City Shopping Centre. Nearby there is also the mega discount store PAK'nSAVE (7am-11pm).

Recommended cheap accommodation

YHA Christchurch

Decent hostel with helpful staff and a large kitchen. YHA also have YHA Rolleston House, but this is a rather old, slightly shabby building. *Private rooms from $88, dorms from $26 (10% off for YHA members) • Tel: 03 366 6564 • 5 Worcester Blvd, Christchurch Central, Christchurch 8013 •* www.yha.co.nz

Jailhouse Accommodation (BBH)

Want to try something a little different and stay the night in an old jail? The unique experience this place provides has won it a host of awards. *Beds from $29 for BBH members, from $33 for non-members • Tel: 03 982 7777 • 338 Lincoln Road, Addington •* www.jail.co.nz

Jucy Snooze

A good option if you have an early flight or are looking for something near the airport, this capsule hotel is reasonably new and has a massive lounge to hang out in. Normal private rooms and family rooms also available. *Capsules from $25, private rooms from $109 • Tel: 0800 427 736 • 5 Peter Leeming Road, Christchurch Airport, Christchurch 8053 •* www.jucysnooze.co.nz

How to get there and away

By bus

The centrally located Christchurch Bus Interchange makes using the bus super easy around the city. InterCity, as well as all the bus tour companies stop off here at least on a daily basis. Additionally, Atomic Travel (www.atomictravel.co.nz) provides direct services to Greymouth (4 hours, $55), via Arthur's Pass and Dunedin (6 hours, $35), via Oamaru (2 hours, $35).

By car or campervan

Christchurch is about three hours from Tekapo and Oamaru, five hours from Dunedin and six hours drive from Queenstown.

By air

Budget airline Jetstar has a bunch of cheap flights to Christchurch, but several other airlines go here so check prices on Skyscanner. The easiest way to get to and from the city center is to take the Purple line bus (30 mins, $8.50 one-way, $15 return).

Tourist information

The i-SITE information center is between the museum and the art gallery (8:30am-5pm).

Sumner Beach

A perfect city getaway on a sunny afternoon, Sumner is a pleasant coastal suburb a short bus or car ride away from central Christchurch. The beach is popular for swimming with its gently sloping sand and lifeguards in summer, which also makes it an excellent place for beginner surfers. Many people like to take a casual stroll down the esplanade, stopping off at the viewpoints along the way. Halfway along the beach is Cave Rock, a huge rocky outcrop with a cave underneath and steps to climb up for that perfect Instagram post! *By bus: from the bus interchange in Christchurch, take the Purple Line to Sumner (20 mins, $4). By car: Sumner is about 20 minutes east from central Christchurch, via Ferry Road, then Main Road*

Christchurch to Queenstown

Lake Tekapo

Lake Tekapo is a stunning turquoise-colored lake surrounded by the grand mountains of the Southern Alps. The township on the southern end of the lake is well set up for most kinds of travelers and is also part of a UNESCO Dark Sky Reserve, meaning it's a great place to come for stargazing. It's definitely worth breaking up a journey from Christchurch to Queenstown by spending a day here, or using it as a base to explore nearby spots such as Mount Cook.

Things to do

All the sights and attractions in Tekapo are walkable from each other, with signs and maps around the village making it very easy to navigate your way around.

Church of the Good Shepherd

You can't come to Tekapo and not get a picture of this quaint little church. Situated along the shores of the lake, the church was built as a memorial to the pioneers who came to the surrounding Mackenzie Country.

Tekapo Springs

Those that have read the Japan guides from Super Cheap Guides will know how numerous hot springs are there, but as another volcanic island country New Zealand also has a few. Using natural water, full of all sorts of minerals for a revitalized body, Tekapo Springs has multiple baths of different temperatures, as well as a sauna. Bring your own towels and swimsuit. *Adults $27, children $17, families $87 • 10am-8pm •* https://tekaposprings.co.nz *• West side of the village*

Mt John Observatory and stargazing

There are some operators in town, such as Tekapo Stargazing (https://tekapostargazing.co.nz) and Earth and Sky (www.earthandsky.co.nz) that provide stargazing tours for $129 and $175 respectively, but many will consider this too pricey, unless they want a detailed rundown of what they are seeing. A free alternative is to just head up in your car to nearby the Mt John Observatory, or ask at your accommodation where the best place to stargaze nearby is. If you're lucky, you may just need to set up your camera on the hostel's terrace to see the stars!

Walk around Lake Tekapo

Take a breathtaking stroll around the lake, in either direction, any time of the year, and you're sure to come back with some mightily impressive photos. Heading around to the west side is probably easiest. *Difficulty: Easy • Time required: routes usually 1-2 hours • Routes start from shore near the village, many are well signposted, but free maps are available at the information center if you'd prefer*

Budget food

While there are plenty of pubs and some slightly expensive restaurants on the main road, there is a cheap bakery and an interesting place to try the local salmon:
Doughboys Bakery and Cafe Restaurant - Reasonably priced pies, sandwiches, cakes, fried breakfasts, burgers and so much more. *Snacks from $3, meals around $10 • 6am-9pm*
Kohan - Try the locally caught salmon, prepared by chefs from Japan. Popular with Asian tourists, it also has Japanese favorites like Udon noodles and Katsu pork. *Meals $12-22 • 11am-2pm, 7pm-9pm • Inside the same building as Aotea Gifts*

Cheap supermarkets

Four Square has a pretty well-equipped store near the main bus terminal and car park (8am-8pm). It also has lots of ready-made and pre-heated meals.

Recommended cheap accommodation

Lake Front Backpackers Lodge
With a large BBQ area and an open fireplace, this hostel is a very pleasant way to spend the night. It's about 10 minutes on foot from the village. *Private rooms from $150, dorms from $42 • Tel: 03 680 6825 • 2 Lakeside Dr, Lake Tekapo 7990 •* https://laketekapo-accommodation.co.nz

YHA Lake Tekapo
This brand new hostel, located right on the lakefront, has been built from the ground up for budget travelers. Rooms are available to suit all kinds of tastes, plus there is a large communal lounge, a BBQ area and a lovely fireplace. *Beds from $35 (10% off for YHA members) • Tel: 03 680 6857 • 5 Motuariki Lane, Lake Tekapo •* www.yha.co.nz

Tailor Made Tekapo Backpackers (BBH)
Family run hostel surrounded by a very picturesque garden. Proper beds, no bunks here. *Beds from $38 (from $34 with BBH card) • Tel: 03 680 6700 • 11 Aorangi Crescent, Lake Tekapo •* www.tekapohostelnz.com

---

How to get there and away

By bus

The cheapest way to get from Queenstown to Christchurch or the other way around is to take a bus with InterCity, which stops off halfway in Lake Tekapo (3-4 hours, usually around $40 either way). Kiwi Experience and Stray also stop off here on the same route.

By car or campervan

Lake Tekapo is about three hours from Christchurch or Queenstown via the highway system, and one hour from Mount Cook (head west and follows signs). There are gas stations on the main road in the village center.

Tourist information

There is a tourist information booth in the Kiwi Treasures store on the main road (8am-7pm).

Mount Cook (Aoraki)

Mount Cook, known as Aoraki in Maori, is the tallest mountain in New Zealand, used by the famous climber Sir Edmund Hillary to hone his skills in preparation for his ascent up Mount Everest. The village nearby is a great spot to base yourself for a hike or two in the surrounding Aoraki Mount Cook National Park, with hiking routes to suit all kinds of fitness levels. It's a super pristine setting, with grand peaks, snow fields present all year round and some mega glaciers to see. If you're lucky, you'll also come across the rather cheeky kea birds, just watch out for your food as they like to grab it!

Things to do

There are several trails around Mount Cook, some of which can be started from the main settlement. Those looking for more challenging hikes, for example on unformed tracks, should check the Department of Conservation website at www.doc.govt.nz. Here are the best for budget travelers spending a day or two in Mount Cook:

Governors Bush Walk
A nice choice for families, this walk provides a good chance to see some local birdlife as well. You'll be walking through the bush and be able to see one of the few silver beech forests still left in the national park, as well as an amazing view of the mountains. *Difficulty: Easy • Time required: 1 hour return • Starts from the public shelter to the west of the village, near Mount Cook Motels*

Kea Point Lookout
Take a gentle walk along boardwalks through subalpine grasslands and scrub before ending up at the lookout. Here you'll be greeted with a spectacular view of Hooker Valley, Mueller Glacier lake and Mount Cook. *Difficulty: Easy • Time required: 2 hours return from village • Trail starts at the Department of Conservation Visitor Centre*

Hooker Valley Track
Heading in the direction of Mount Cook, this well-known track passes many excellent viewpoints. Along the way you'll pass over a few swing bridges as you cross over Hooker River and various local wildflower spots. At the end you'll be rewarded with a view of the glacial

lake. If you can, start walking this track at dawn to see the stunning sunrise view over the mountains. *Difficulty: Medium • Time required: 4 hours return from the village (3 hours if you start at the parking lot up the road from the village) • Trail starts from the Department of Conservation Visitor Centre*

Budget food

It's slim pickings in Mount Cook, so definitely bring food with you from your previous destination, such as from the Four Square supermarket in Lake Tekapo.

Recommended cheap accommodation

Mount Cook Backpackers
Modern complex with dorm rooms and motel units for families or large groups. Be sure to check out the 'Peak Deals' section on their site for the latest discounts. *Private rooms from $165, dorms from $48 • Tel: 0800 100 512 • Bowen Dr, Mount Cook National Park 7999 •* www.mountcookbackpackers.co.nz

Aoraki Alpine Lodge
Another perfect place to spend the night in Mount Cook, this lodge has even more types of rooms, plus apartments. *Private rooms from $149, whole bunk rooms from $185 • Tel: 03 435 1860 • 101 Bowen Drive, Mount Cook Village 7946 •* https://aorakialpinelodge.co.nz

YHA Aoraki Mt Cook
Stay here if you have a YHA card and want to get that lovely 10% discount. Like the others it has a cozy lounge and mountain views. *Private rooms from $140, dorms from $38 (10% off for YHA members) • Tel: 03 435 1820 • 4 Bowen Drive, Mt Cook Village •* www.yha.co.nz

How to get there and away

By bus

The Cook Connection (www.cookconnect.co.nz) provide a shuttle bus from Lake Tekapo (90 mins, return $75). InterCity also run tour buses, but it's usually quite pricey (80 mins, $90). Stray and Kiwi Experience can also take you here.

By car or campervan

Mount Cook is about one hour from Lake Tekapo. Just head down State Highway 8 and turn right when you see the sign. Going south, it's around three hours to Queenstown.

Tourist information

The National Park Visitor Centre is on Larch Grove Road (8:30am-4:30pm).

Stop-off point: Omarama

There's not much to do in Omarama, but as it's almost halfway between Lake Tekapo and Queenstown or Wanaka, it's a convenient stop-off point to grab some food and stretch the legs. As well as some pubs, there are a few spots for a cheap meal near where State Highways 8 and 83 connect. Note that InterCity buses stop right outside the below cafe.
Merino Country Cafe - Friendly cafe and gift shop, with classic roadside station foods like cooked breakfasts, sandwiches and pies. *Meals $6-12 • 8:30am-5pm (until 4pm in winter)*
Four Square - As well as the usual supermarket items, they have pastries and sandwiches. *Snacks $2-4, light meals $4-8 • 8am-7pm*

Queenstown

Queenstown is the extreme sports and adventure capital of New Zealand, if not the world. The birthplace of jetboats and bungy jumping, the large town offers an almost countless number of activities. It also has more relaxing pursuits, such as hiking and an excellent gondola, many of which are free or a short drive or bus ride away from town. But with all that's on offer, it's quite easy to burn your savings away in Queenstown, so always use the deals on offer and never be afraid to haggle!

Getting around

Queenstown has recently updated its bus network, and it's suddenly become one of the best for tourists in New Zealand. One of the first things those without a car should do is to get an Orbus GoCard card from the airport, a bus driver or O'Connell's Shopping Centre in town. With this card all bus rides will have a flat rate of just $2, compared to $5 if you use cash. You'll soon start to save a bit, even if you are in Queenstown for just a few days. The bus lines are color-coded and easy to follow, with regular buses on most routes. Buses can sometimes be late though, so make sure you plan to get an early one if heading to the airport.

Discount tickets and combos

Your first port of call should be www.bookme.co.nz, which collects together many of the town's deals, with some pretty unbelievably low prices on offer. If you find a preferred operator, make sure you check their official website too, as they may offer exclusive deals if you buy direct from them. For example, while tour operator Real Journeys can seem expensive, they sometimes offer 20% off additional tours and kids-go-free offers.

When in town, exploring the local travel agents is a good idea it if you have time. Agents such as Happy Travels and Peterpans can offer some excellent deals, while Queenstown Combos are also worth heading into. Also note that many staff at tour operators in town, while it's not officially known to the public, are actually able to offer you a discount if you haggle. It may depend on the staff member serving you, so never be afraid to be a little pushy or come back later and try to get another staff member to give you a better deal!

Things to do

Central Queenstown

Skyline Gondola

Head up the gondola for amazing panoramic views of Queenstown and the surrounding alpine mountains. At the top kids and big kids can enjoy a surprisingly enjoyable luge ride, grab a beer or just walk around taking pictures. It's also possible to walk up in about one hour instead of paying for the expensive gondola, via the Tiki Trail. Just head left at the gondola station and follow the signs. *Gondola from $39, with luge rides from $55, family deals from $113 • 9am-9pm •* www.skyline.co.nz *• Short walk north from the city center*

Hike to Ben Lomond

The iconic hike in Queenstown, the Ben Lomond summit has been the number one spot to hike to since the British came all those years back. Heading through forest and around mountain valleys, it's a must do in Queenstown. If heading to the summit seems a bit scary or is too much on your legs, you can just head to the Ben Lomond Saddle, which is just before you really climb up to the summit. Splendid views any time of the year. *Difficulty: Medium • Time required: 4-6 hours • Starts from the top of the Skyline Gondola, so can be combined with the Tiki Trail*

The spectacular view from Ben Lomond Saddle as you approach the summit of Ben Lomond

Queenstown Gardens

This quiet garden, especially beautiful when the autumn leaves are out, is a lovely place to chill out in. It's also popular for a spot of frisbee throwing, with some devilishly difficult targets. There are also tennis courts and an ice rink if you have children to keep busy. *FREE • 24h*

TSS Earnslaw Steamship Cruise
An excellent way to see Queenstown and the surrounding landscape, this cruise around Lake Wakatipu is the most popular attraction in town. Using an authentic coal-fired steamship, it's quite a luxurious experience. This unfortunately means high prices, so make sure you check www.realjourneys.co.nz/en/plan/specials/ for any deals that are currently on. *Adults from $70, children from $30 • Various times throughout the day (not operational early June to early July) •* www.realjourneys.co.nz

Spirit of Queenstown Scenic Cruise
If you feel the TSS Earnslaw is too expensive, then the Southern Discoveries cruise might be a better option. It uses a similar route, but takes guests on a modern catamaran boat rather than an old steamship. Discounts available on their official website. *Adults from $45, children from $25 • Various times throughout the day •* www.southerndiscoveries.co.nz

One Mile Creek Trail
Leading up along a creek, this walk takes you through native beech forest, past an old hydro plant and up to the track for Ben Lomond. At this point you can either return or proceed up to Ben Lomond. One of the quieter hikes in town. *Difficulty: Medium • Time required: 2 hours return • Starts from the roundabout down the road from YHA Lakefront, just before the road goes up to Fernhill*

Queenstown Hill
Offering similar views to the top of the gondola but away from the tour buses and most tourists, this hike is a good choice for an afternoon hike. *Difficulty: Medium • Time required: 3-4 hours return • Starts from the east side of town. Follow signs to the trail entrance*

Minus 5° ICE BAR
Super fun experience on a night out. Note some tour operators in town give out 10% off vouchers to customers. *Adults from $25, children from $15 • 2pm-11pm •* www.minus5icebar.com

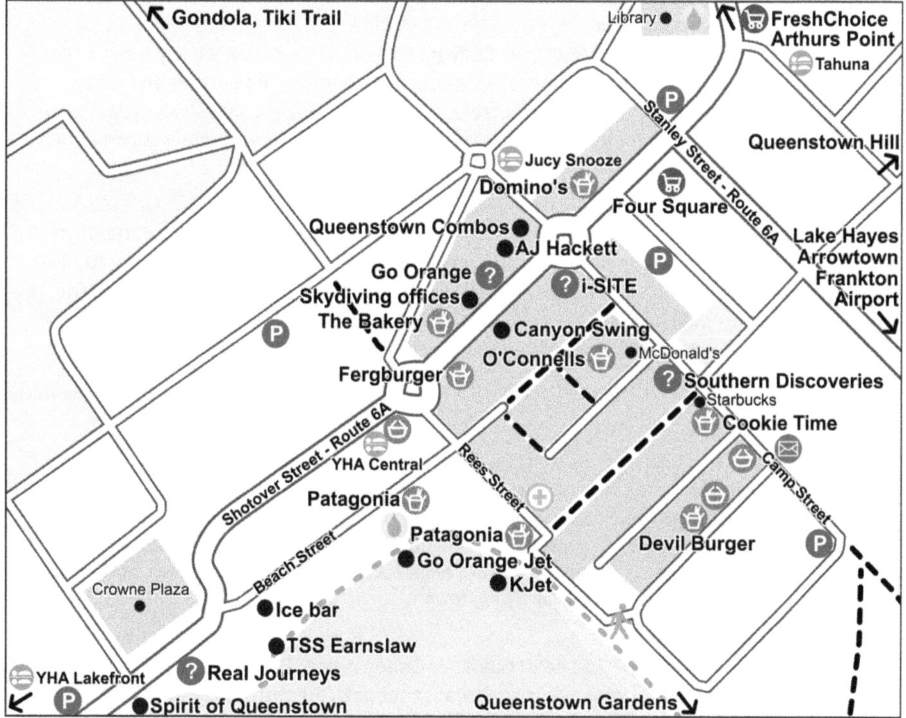

Extreme sports and activities

It would take 100 pages to list all the activities on offer and the various providers, and the list is always growing, so here are the best and most popular activities for budget travelers:

Bungy Jumping with AJ Hackett Bungy

How could you come to Queenstown and not do a bungy jump? AJ Hackett offers a variety of jumps. At 43 meters Kawarau Bridge is best for beginners or those who are most nervous, and also offers a dunk in the water for those that want it! The Nevis Bungy is the ultimate jump though, at a height of 134 meters. Various swing and zipride experiences are also on offer at these destinations, with combo savings on offer. *Adults from $205, children from $155 • 9:30am-4:30pm • www.bungy.co.nz • Free shuttle buses depart from AJ Hackett office in Queenstown*

Skydiving

There are a few providers in town, so have a look around before deciding. NZONE does their dives near Queenstown, so is the most popular but doesn't have the best scenery (from $299). Skydive Southern Alps departs from the town of Glenorchy 30 minutes away and has arguably the better scenery as you descend (from $289). There is also skydiving in Wanaka with Skydive Wanaka (from $299). Prices are higher the higher you jump from, but 9000ft is enough for most people. All operators provide shuttle buses from Queenstown to the launch sites.

Jetboating

There are a variety of companies offering jetboating, all aimed at different audiences. Those looking for a quick, cheap ride should check out Go Orange (adults $79, children $39), or KJet if they want a longer ride from the town center (adults $135, children $69, families $307). If you're looking for a more adventurous experience through narrower ravines and valleys, then go for Shotover Jet (adults $155, children $89, families $399). They also offer a free shuttle bus from their office in town to Arthurs Point, where the boats depart from.

Shotover Canyon Swing and Fox

Have fun jumping or swinging off Shotover Canyon. Run off, cycle off on a baby tricycle, get your friend to kick you off the edge; there are a countless number of hilarious and crazy options. Combo and group savings are available. *Canyon Fox jump from $169, Canyon Swing from $249 • Various times throughout the day • www.canyonswing.co.nz • Free shuttle buses depart from the Shotover Canyon Swing office in Queenstown*

Rafting

An exhilarating activity for those that want a more physical experience. The two operators, Go Orange and Challenge Rafting, both take customers down Shotover River and Kawarau River. Kawarau River is best for first timers as Shotover River can become a bit too energetic for some. *Both operators from $199 • Various times throughout the day • www.raft.co.nz and www.goorange.co.nz • Both offer shuttle buses from Queenstown*

Outside of town

Lake Hayes

Take a relaxing walk or bike ride around this large lake. Usually devoid of tourists, it's more of a spot for locals. Unlike other lakes in the area extreme water sports are not allowed here, so you can enjoy the pristine views and shimmering waters in peace. *Difficulty: Easy • Time required: 1-2 hours on foot, 45 mins on bike • By bus: from Queenstown, take the bus bound for Arrowtown and stop off at Amisfield Winery (30 mins). Be sure to note bus times back, as they can finish earlier than other routes. By car: 15 minutes up State Highway 6 from town*

Cycle the Queenstown Trail

There are various cycling trails that head out from Queenstown. The main one is the Queenstown Trail, a series of mostly off-road trails that link Queenstown with Arrowtown and the Gibbston Valley wine country. Along the way you can drop in at some wineries and cafes for refreshment. Bike rental companies can arrange shuttle buses if you only want to do a certain section. Around The Basin (www.aroundthebasin.co.nz) and Vertigo Bikes (http://vertigobikes.co.nz) come recommended by fellow travelers, with bike rental starting from around $25. Check their websites for current deals on offer.

Arrowtown

A historic, charming village near Queenstown, Arrowtown is an old gold rush spot and a worthwhile side trip. Take a stroll around the village center, full of gold rush era buildings, then head to one of the below attractions. Note there is a Night 'n Day convenience store in the village center if you need any cheap food or drinks.

Lakes District Museum

Built within three of the village's old gold rush era buildings, this museum is full of interesting displays and more on Arrowtown's rich history. Visitors can also have fun dressing up in traditional costumes. *Adults $10, children $3, under five FREE • 8:30am-5pm •* www.museumqueenstown.com *• In the center of the village*

Historic Arrowtown Chinese Settlement

During the gold rush many Chinese people came over to make a living, and settled in the area. Come here to see the kinds of places they lived in and what life was like for them. *FREE • 24h • Follow signs from the center of the village*

Discount stores

Outside of Queenstown, near the airport, is a big branch of The Warehouse (7am-12am), which has cheap travel items, such as hiking gear, swimsuits and suitcases.

Budget food

Fergburger - There's always a long line at what has been described by many as the best burger joint in New Zealand. Don't listen to grumbling locals who don't go here because of the wait, it's the real deal and worth the price. The bakery next door is also good if you need a coffee and breakfast before an early departing tour. *Burgers from $12 • 8am-5am*

Devil Burger - Line too long at Fergburger? This alternative burger restaurant and takeout has an inventive menu and great service. *Burgers from $11 • 10am-3am*

Domino's - Ok, hardly an authentic New Zealand culinary experience, but for prices this low, how can you say no when you're super hungry! *Pizzas from $5 when ordered online, from $6 when ordered at the store • 11am-Midnight*

The Bakery Queenstown - Traditional bakery with reasonable prices for Queenstown. Buy one get one free from 5pm to 6pm. *Pies and snacks $3-5 • 6am-6pm*

O'Connell's Shopping Centre - Downstairs is a food court with Asian food, McDonald's, Indian food and cheap kebabs. Prices are still higher than outside Queenstown, but good for this town. *Meals from around $10 • 9am-9pm*

Cookie Time - Freshly baked cookies and some mouth-watering smoothies and hot chocolates. Note the deals on the board at the entrance before going in, as they have buy one, get one free deals and $1 coffees in the mornings. *Cookies $4-5 • 8am-10pm*

Patagonia Chocolates - Another real indulgence, Patagonia's ice creams are to die for. *Ice creams and chocolates $4-7 • 9am-9pm (until 8pm on Sundays)*

Chur Fish and Chips - Super fresh fish, friendly service and a retro arcade machine to play while you wait. How could it get any better? Definitely worth heading here if you are in Fernhill to the west of town. *Meals from around $8-10 • 12pm-9pm (from 4pm Mondays and Tuesdays) • Up Fernhill Road, next to the Eight To Late convenience store*

Cheap supermarkets

In the town center is Four Square (7am-10pm). A 10 minute walk or short drive north up the road is FreshChoice (7am-11pm), a reasonably large supermarket with decent prices. Outside of town, in Frankton there is a branch of the mega cheap supermarket PAK'nSAVE (7am-10pm), just north of the airport. Buses here are infrequent, so it may be a bit of a waste of time coming here if you don't have a car.

Recommended cheap accommodation

YHA Queenstown Lakefront Backpackers
Rebuilt not long ago, this excellent hostel has a variety of rooms and also offers special discounts on some tours to guests. *Beds from $30 (10% off for YHA members) • 88-90 Lake Esplanade, Queenstown 9300 • Tel: 03 442 8413 •* www.yha.co.nz

Jucy Snooze
Jucy has opened a new hotel that resembles the capsule hotels in Japan (see the Super Cheap Japan book if you are visiting there too!). Everyone sleeps in little pods, meaning there is an element of privacy, plus there is a large kitchen space and areas to relax in. *Capsules from $33 • Tel: 03 927 4204 • 47 Camp Street, Queenstown 9300 •* www.jucysnooze.co.nz

Tahuna Pod Hostel
Prices may seem a little higher here than elsewhere, but the free breakfast and soup in the evenings, plus free entry to the ice bar, are a cool bonus for budget travelers. Private rooms as well as pods are available to sleep in. *Beds from $31 a night • Tel: 03 442 7052 • 11 Henry Street, Queenstown 9300 •* www.tahunapodhostel.co.nz

---

How to get there and away

By bus

All the major bus companies, such as InterCity, Stray and Kiwi stop off or have hubs in Queenstown, so it's very easy to get to by bus. Tracknet also provides transportation to and from Queenstown to less frequented places, as well as Invercargill, Manapouri (for Doubtful Sound) and various starting points for hiking trails. Book at https://tracknet.net.

By car or campervan

Queenstown is around two hours from Te Anau, two and a half hours from Invercargill, just over two hours from Manapouri (Doubtful Sound) and four to five hours from Milford Sound. There are many gas stations around town and in nearby Frankton as you head east.

By air

Good old Jetstar has lots of flights to this resort town, with flights from Australia as well as Auckland and Wellington. Qantas, Air New Zealand and Virgin Australia also fly here from more than a dozen locations, but it's usually cheaper to travel by bus if you're already on the South Island. As mentioned, take the local bus into town (15 mins, $2).

Free Wifi

There is a free Wifi service in town, but it's not very reliable. Good alternatives for free Wifi access are Starbucks, Cookie Time and McDonald's.

Tourist information

The i-SITE Visitor Information Centre is located in the center of town (8:30am-9pm).

Around Queenstown

Wanaka

The peaceful Wanaka lakefront

Wanaka could be considered to be Queenstown's little brother. It still has all the essentials you'll need as a budget traveler, but it's just a smaller and usually quieter place to visit. Therefore some travelers actually prefer Wanaka, as they consider Queenstown to feel too commercialized. Located at the southern end of Lake Wanaka, it's also a convenient starting point for those wanting to explore the Mount Aspiring National Park.

Things to do

Wanaka Lakefront

Grab an ice cream or drink from one of the convenience stores or ice cream shops and head down to the beach on the lakefront. It's the perfect place to lay down and take it easy for an hour or two. The views are rather lovely too. Kayaks and 'Stand Up Paddle Boards' can be rented as well (from $20).

Skydive Wanaka

While you can also do it via Queenstown, for those in Wanaka this company is best. Various heights are available, with prices getting rather high as well, so be careful! People that just want to watch their friends dive from the ground can also come along. Check the special deals section on their website, as well as BookMe before booking. *From $299 • 6:30am-4:30pm • Wanaka Airport, Mustang Lane, Wanaka •* www.skydivewanaka.com

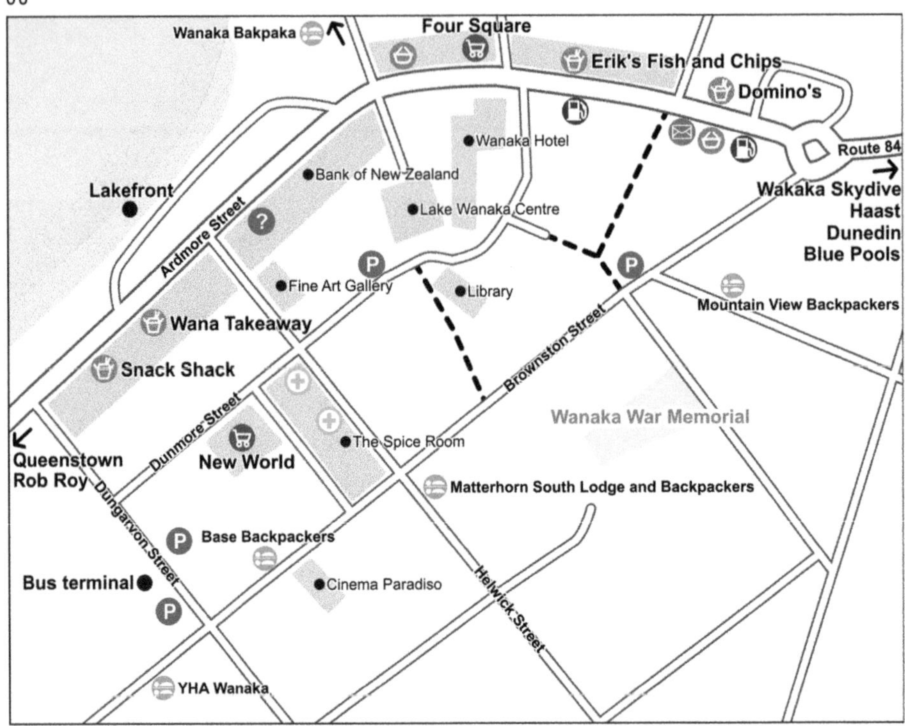

Mount Aspiring National Park

New Zealand's third largest national park, and part of a World Heritage Area, Mount Aspiring National Park has more than 50 species of birds, three of the largest glaciers in the region and many hiking tracks to investigate. If you're a hardcore hiker looking for an extreme challenge, head to the local Department of Conservation office. Otherwise, we recommend these tracks:

Blue Pools and Isthmus Peak Track

Worth stopping off at if heading up the west coast. Suitable for all ages and fitness levels, this popular track will take you through the silver beech forest via boardwalks to the luminous blue pools and an overlooking swing bridge. While probably against the rules, people love to jump off into the water from the bridge. Those looking for something more adventurous should consider walking up Isthmus Peak. *Difficulty: Easy • Time required: Around 1 hour • By car: walk starts at the carpark 8km from the town of Makarora along the Haast Highway (SH6). By bus: transport can be arranged with Wanaka Track Transport at* https://bluepools.co.nz *(1 hour, $70)*

Rob Roy Glacier

A more challenging track, and also cheaper to get to, the Rob Roy Glacier track is a rite of passage for any Wanaka local. Heading into lush beech forest, the track then climbs through a gorge, up into an area of alpine vegetation and finally arrives at a stunning view of Rob Roy Glacier. *Difficulty: Medium • Time required: 4-5 hours return to the bush line and glacier viewpoint • By car: head to the Raspberry Creek Car Park, a one hour drive west from Wanaka, along the Wanaka-Mount Aspiring Road. By bus: transport can be arranged with Ritchies at* www.ritchies.co.nz/wanaka *(1 hour, $20)*

Budget food

While it's always cheaper to cook for yourself in a town like Wanaka, there are some nice options for those that want to eat out, or grab a bite and chill on the beach.

Snack Shack Turkish Kebabs - Cheap kebabs, burgers and ice creams. *Meals $10-14 • 11am-8:30pm*
Wana Takeaway - Perfect for a quick bite and a coffee, or some very tasty fish and chips. *Meals $8-12 • Irregular times*
Erik's Fish and Chips - Increasingly popular food truck business selling the best fish and chips in town. *Meal deals $10, fish from $6 • 12pm-8pm*
Domino's - Only worth heading to if you just have $5 left and an empty belly! Order online for the best prices. *Pizzas from $5 when ordered online • 11am-11pm*

Cheap supermarkets

The best prices can usually be found at New World (7am-9pm) on Dunmore Street. There is also a Four Square on the main street, Ardmore Street, which is open a little later (7am-10pm).

Recommended cheap accommodation

Wanaka Bakpaka

Overlooking Lake Wanaka, this hostel has all sorts of rooms, and would be good for both independent travelers and families. A little away from town, it's in a relatively quiet setting. *Private rooms from $66, dorms from $32 • Tel: 03 443 7837 • 117 Lakeside Road, Wanaka 9305 •* www.wanakabakpaka.co.nz

YHA Wanaka

More centrally located is the local YHA. Spacious and with a great lounge to chill out in and play a bit of pool, it's a safe choice. *Beds from $33 (10% off for YHA members) • Tel: 03 443 1880 • 94 Brownston Street, Wanaka •* www.yha.co.nz

---

How to get there and away

By bus

InterCity usually have the cheapest shuttle buses from and to Queenstown (2 hours, $20-$30). Ritchies also provide buses if InterCity are sold out, but they tend to be pricier. On the other hand, Ritchies have the added bonus of free drop-off at your accommodation, rather than just at a central hub. Both go to Queenstown Airport. Ritchies also has coaches from Cromwell (40 mins, $20) and Dunedin (4 hours, $50). InterCity goes to the west coast, as well as offering a bunch of connections to other towns and cities.

By car or campervan

Wanaka is about one hour from Queenstown (via Cardrona Valley Road), 40 minutes from Cromwell and around one hour from Clyde and Alexandra. Dunedin is three to four hours away. There is a BP gas station in the center of town.

Free Wifi

New World supermarket has free wifi, as does Wanaka Library (10am-5:30pm, closed Sundays). There are also some Spark phone boxes around town that have wifi functionality, which can be used by Spark customers.

Tourist information

The Wanaka i-SITE Visitor Information Centre is located on the lakefront (9am-6pm).

Te Anau

Te Anau is the last main town before heading into Milford Sound. It's not quite as hip as Queenstown but still has all the basics you need as a budget traveler, from a large supermarket to a good selection of hostels. It's therefore a perfect spot to stock up on food and drinks before heading into the Fiordland National Park. In a way, you could call Te Anau a mini-Queenstown. It doesn't have any of the latter's glitz and glam, but the relaxing setting with the mountains across the lake is truly mind-blowing.

Things to do

Te Anau Glowworm Caves

While the caves in Waitomo are most famous, the Te Anau Glowworm Caves experience is more intimate and less touristy. Guests enter underground limestone caves, walking past rushing water underneath before entering little boats. They are then taken to see the glowworms, with thousands shimmering above in complete darkness, and utter silence. Excellent tour guides provide extra information and can answer any questions you may have. Tickets are a little pricey, so if you want to do the glowworm caves it's best to also book something else with Real Journeys, so you can use their 20% Multi Saver discount, which gives 20% off the lower priced tour(s) when booked together. Check out all their deals at www.realjourneys.co.nz/en/plan/specials. *Adults from $98, children from $30 • Various departure times, with several departures in peak season • Departs from the Real Journeys Visitor Centre*

Book your Milford Sound and Doubtful Sound cruises

Both Real Journeys and Southern Discoveries have offices in town if you want to book while in Te Anau. See the Milford and Doubtful Sound chapters for more information.

Kepler Track

This self-guided tour is an excellent option for budget travelers, especially if there are no spaces to do the Milford Track. Also a New Zealand official Great Walk, the Kepler Track starts from the quiet shores of Lake Te Anau, then takes you via some pristine forests to the summit of Mount Luxmore, which offers some truly amazing alpine views. Hut and camping site spots must be booked beforehand with the Department of Conservation at www.doc.govt.nz, which also lists shuttle buses for those who don't have a car and boat options if needed, plus detailed hiking maps.. *Difficulty: Medium • Time required: 3-4 days • Main entrance is from the Kepler Track car park, to the southern end of Lake Te Anau, about 5 km from the actual town*

Bird Sanctuary

If you have a bit of free time or want to do a less taxing walk than the Kepler Track, heading around the lake to the bird sanctuary is a nice diversion. A wide selection of local birds are on show, including the famous kea birds, so it's also a great place to keep the kids occupied for a bit. *FREE • 24h • Walk south down the bay for around 45 minutes (see map)*

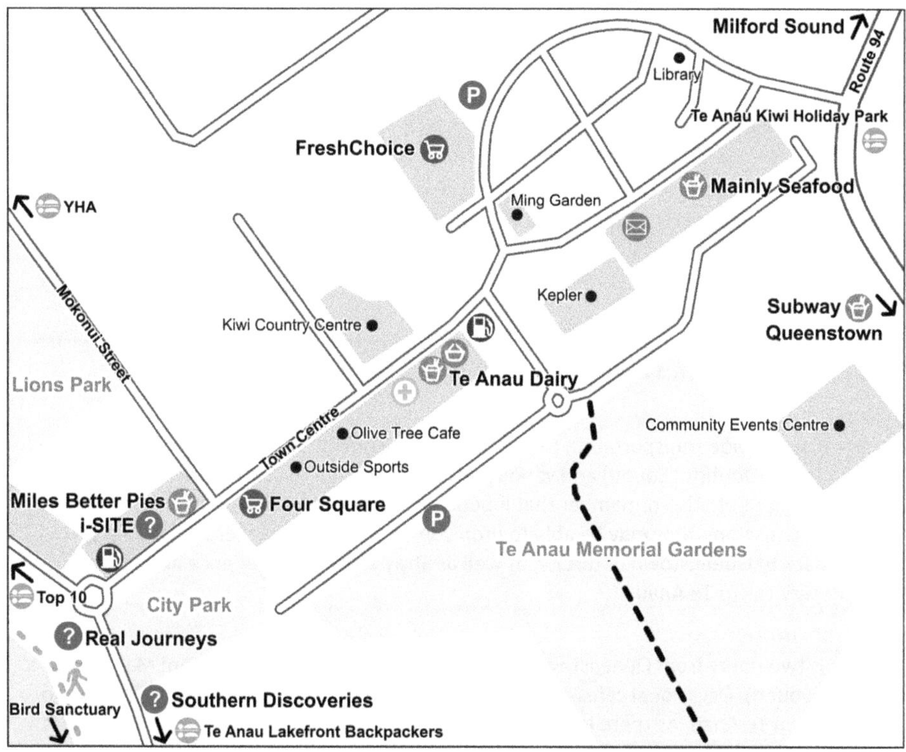

Budget food

As well as a few pubs and Chinese restaurants, there is a decent collection of places to eat for budget travelers in the center of town:

Miles Better Pies - Delicious homemade pies, soups and deep-fried snacks. *Pies from $5, sandwiches from $6.5 • 6am-6pm (October to May)*

Te Anau Dairy - Offers Chinese dishes as well as fish and chips, plus standard convenience store items. *Meals $8-12 • 10am-10pm*

Mainly Seafood - Classic fish and chip joint that also has some pretty mega burgers. *Meals $6-10 • 4:30pm-9pm*

Subway - Branch of the international sandwich chain, and a good choice if other places are closed. *Sandwiches from $5 • 7am-9pm*

Cheap supermarkets

Four Square (7:30am-8pm) is OK, but the FreshChoice down the road (7am-9pm) is much larger, and usually cheaper. You can also get some travel essentials in these stores, such as chargers and cables.

Recommended cheap accommodation

YHA Te Anau Backpacker Hostel

A variety of private and dorm room options are available here, so it should be able to suit most tastes. Has a large kitchen with plenty of space to relax, as well as a hot room in which to dry your clothes for free. *Beds from $31 (10% off for YHA members) • Tel: 03 249 7847 • 29 Mokonui Street, Te Anau 9600 •* www.yha.co.nz

Bob and Maxine's Backpackers

This BBH hostel is a little out of town, so best if you have your own mode of transportation. A modern lodge with free wifi and bicycle rental, plus reasonably spacious rooms. *Beds from $40 (from $36 with BBH card) • Tel: 03 249 8006 / 03 249 8066 • 80, Mount York Road, Rainbow Downs, Lake Te Anau 9600 •* www.barnyardbackpackers.com

Te Anau Top 10 Holiday Park

This well-regarded chain is a big hit with families. Playgrounds, a BBQ area and a recreation room are among the many facilities on offer here. *Sites from $23, dorms from $30, private rooms from $90 • Tel: 03 249 8538 • 15 Luxmore Dr, Te Anau 9600 •* https://top10.co.nz/park/te-anau-top-10-holiday-park

---

How to get there and away

By bus

Tracknet can provide transportation to and from Queenstown, as well as Invercargill, Manapouri (for Doubtful Sound) and various starting points for hiking trails. Book at https://tracknet.net. Also remember that if booking a cruise in Milford Sound or Doubtful Sound, the cruise operator may be able to drop you off here after, rather than taking you all the way back to Queenstown. InterCity, as well as Stray and Kiwi Experience also have frequent services to Te Anau.

By car or campervan

Te Anau is two hours from Queenstown or Invercargill, or just 30 minutes from Manapouri (Doubtful Sound). Occasional cafes and shops are located along the way. There are also two gas stations in Te Anau. As there is officially no gas station in Milford Sound, this is your last place to fill up!

Free Wifi

The tiny Te Anau Library has free wifi (8:30am-5pm, until 3pm Saturdays, closed Sundays), otherwise it's best to grab wifi at a cafe or at your accommodation.

Tourist information

There is a centrally located i-SITE in town (8:30am-7pm), which can provide impartial advice on what to do in Te Anau, as well as various excursions from town.

Milford Sound

Milford Sound is the most popular way to see the Fiordland National Park, New Zealand's most famous, and possibly the most stunning place in the country. Combining grand mountain peaks, huge waterfalls and sheer cliffs hundreds of meters high, Milford Sound is a must visit for most budget travelers. It's a bit of a mission to get there, but any local will assure you that it will be worth it as soon as you see the fjord for the first time.

During the summer, try to go for an early departing cruise, as they are far less crowded than the afternoon ones. Note that the road to Milford Sound can sometimes be blocked due to avalanche or heavy rain warnings, so it's best not to book a Milford Sound cruise on your last day in Queenstown or Te Anau.

Discount tickets and combos

Some tour operators offer amazing discounts when booking more than one tour at the same time, such as Real Journeys, who offer 20% off the cheaper tours. Most cruise companies will also offer combo tour savings, so ask if they also offer other activities you want to try. Tour resellers, especially Happy Travels in Queenstown, also offer great deals if you buy more than one tour with them. Try to haggle and you might get a better price! As ever, check Bookme.co.nz, where you can save up to 60% on cruises at Milford Sound.

Things to do

All the cruise companies in Milford Sound take approximately the same route around the fjord, with the exception of overnight cruises and Real Journeys Nature Cruise. Most also offer transport from Queenstown or Te Anau. You can either join a tour via coach from Queenstown or Te Anau, or drive there yourselves.

Cruise companies

Real Journeys

Some of the most modern boats and excellent service. Their Nature Cruise is the best, as it uses a larger boat that can go out a little bit into the Tasman Sea. While Real Journeys might seem the most expensive option, they have plenty of deals, such as 'Kids go free', at www.realjourneys.co.nz/en/plan/specials. One bonus with Real Journeys is that they offer free pick-ups from your accommodation. If you book with Real Journeys or Go Orange and the road is blocked, they may be able to transfer you to a Doubtful Sound cruise. *Cruise only: Adults from $80, children $30. Cruise with return coach from Queenstown: Adults from $199, children $100. Cruise with return coach from Te Anau: Adults $149, children $75 •* www.realjourneys.co.nz/en

Go Orange

Using the old boats of Real Journeys, this company is the most popular choice with backpackers due to the low prices, but that certainly doesn't mean you'll get an inferior cruise. Go Orange also offer fun kayak tours, which you can do in combination with a cruise. *Cruise only: Adults from $55, children $25. Cruise with return coach from Queenstown: Adults from $139, children $89. Cruise with return coach from Te Anau: Adults $119, children $89 •* www.goorange.co.nz/en

Southern Discoveries

If Real Journeys is Coca-Cola, then Southern Discoveries is Pepsi. Not as big, but always aiming to outdo their main rival, they offer similar, if sometimes inferior quality tours. Prices are therefore sometimes a little cheaper and most cruises include free buffet lunch, so consider this when comparing the cost with other operators. *Cruise only: Adults from $46, children $25. Cruise with return coach from Queenstown: Adults from $189, children $99. Cruise with return coach from Te Anau: Adults $149, children $79 •* www.southerndiscoveries.co.nz

Jucy Cruise

The new boys in town, Jucy offer cruises on their new premium boats as well as a more standard catamaran boat cruise. Special prices are given to those that also rent a car with Jucy. *Cruise only: Adults from $45, children $15, under 5 FREE. Cruise with return coach from Queenstown: Adults from $125, children $75, under 5 FREE •* www.jucycruise.co.nz

Mitre Peak Cruises

This outfit has the smallest boats, meaning you'll have a more intimate experience, but prices will probably be higher unless you do some sort of combo. *Cruise only: Adults from $80, children $25. Cruise with return coach from Queenstown: Adults from $189, children $139. Cruise with return coach from Te Anau: Adults $140, children $89 •* www.mitrepeak.com

Making your own way and joining a cruise tour at Milford Sound

If you decide to drive there yourselves, just put Milford Sound into your satnav and head to the end of the road. From Queenstown (4 hours) or Te Anau (2 hours) the roads are all paved. Along the way, consider stopping off at the serene Mirror Lakes, Knobs Flat for a chance to see the intelligent kea birds and The Divide, where a short hiking trail called Key Summit Track (3 hours) starts, which has awesome panoramic views over the mountains and alpine lakes.

Budget food

Southern Discoveries have a small cafe, but it's best to bring lunch to save on the expensive cruise meals, unless food is included with your cruise.

Recommended cheap accommodation

While there is a lodge at Milford Sound, it's not for those on a budget and is often booked up. Almost everyone does Milford Sound as a day trip, or an overnight cruise via Real Journeys.

Doubtful Sound

Doubtful Sound is a fjord located in the same national park as Milford Sound. Three times longer than Milford Sound and with a surface area ten times as large, it's full of unexpected twists and turns. Along the way you'll see lush rainforest, rugged peaks and, if you are very lucky, you'll be able to see dolphins, fur seals and penguins.

So, which should you do, Milford Sound or Doubtful Sound? If you can only do one, which is best? Well, due to it being even more of a journey to get to Doubtful Sound, it's much less touristy (only two tour companies operate day tours), but this does mean much higher prices. In terms of the scenery, Milford Sound is more mountainous, meaning you'll get a more classic fjord experience with tall waterfalls and steep, high mountains. Doubtful Sound has low, rolling mountains and is much more peaceful, but will still impress most visitors, and you'll have a better chance of seeing wildlife.

If you want to do both Milford Sound and Doubtful Sound, or for example want to be picked up in Queenstown and dropped off in Te Anau, most tour companies should be able to arrange this for you. You may not be able to do this via their website, so send them an email for such requests.

Discount tickets and combos

As with Milford Sound, cruise operators like Go Orange will be offering discounts to those that book directly with them or may offer combo tour savings. Queenstown tour resellers and Bookme.co.nz will also offer some great deals, but probably less so than the easier-to-access and more popular Milford Sound.

Things to do

Tours to Doubtful Sound actually start from a town called Manapouri. From here tourists are taken across Lake Manapouri, then probably one of the world's most spectacular coach trips as they go through Wilmot Pass, from where the beautiful Doubtful Sound appears as you head through the rainforest. Once at Doubtful Sound, you'll start the actual cruise.

Cruise companies

Real Journeys

The Doubtful Sound Wilderness Cruises from Real Journeys offers a three-hour tour of the fjord on a rather posh, modern boat. Superb commentary is provided by the onboard nature guide, who was happy to answer any questions we had. There is a small kiosk on the boats to buy snacks, plus free tea and coffee. *Cruise package from Manapouri: Adults from $259, children $80. Cruise with return coach from Queenstown: Adults from $325, children $163. Cruise with return coach from Te Anau: Adults $279, children $85 •* www.realjourneys.co.nz/en

Go Orange

Go Orange has much smaller boats and lower prices for adults, plus their three-hour cruises also come with expert guides. Note that there is no food available to purchase on the Go Orange boats. As with Milford Sound, they also have excellent kayak tours of different lengths and difficulties. *Cruise package from Manapouri: Adults $229, children $119. Cruise with return coach from Queenstown: Adults $259, children $139. Cruise with return coach from Te Anau: Adults $229, children $119 • Operates 1st October - 30th April •* www.goorange.co.nz/en

Making your own way and joining a cruise tour at Manapouri

Those driving to Manapouri should check in at the Manapouri Visitor Centre, which has free parking (Waiau Street, Pearl Harbour, Manapouri 9643). From Queenstown (around 3 hours) or Te Anau (30 mins), there are occasional cafes to rest at and grab a snack on the way. You can also book bus transportation separately with Tracknet at https://tracknet.net.

Budget food

Real Journeys have a little cafe that sells sandwiches, drinks and ice creams for purchase before cruise departures, but it's a little pricey, so bring some food with you if you can. Again, food pre-booked from the cruise companies is pretty expensive for what you get. Manapouri Cafe & Dairy is also a good choice, with reasonably priced meals and snacks (7:30am-8pm), located around the corner from the Real Journeys office (29 Waiau Street, Manapouri 9679).

Recommended cheap accommodation

While there is some accommodation in Manapouri, you'll find far more budget options in Te Anau, which is only 30 minutes away by car. Note there is no public transportation between the two towns, but it shouldn't be too hard to hitchhike with all the tourists driving through.

Manapouri Motorhome and Caravan Park

A very warm and friendly place to stay the night. Lots of communal areas to hang out in, such as a BBQ area and a children's playground. They can also get Real Journeys to pick you up for free if you book via this accommodation. *Sites from $20 • Tel: 027 249 7669 • 170 Hillside Manapouri Road, Manapouri, Fiordland, RD1 Te Anau, 9679 •* www.manapourirvpark.nz

Barnyard Backpackers (BBH)

Part of the BBH network of hostels, this lovely hostel is located between Manapouri and Te Anau. Set in a deer farm, it has a cozy dining area with a wood fire and a variety of room types. *Beds from $30 (from $28 with BBH card) • Tel: 03 249 8006 / 03 249 8066 • 80, Mount York Road, Rainbow Downs, Lake Te Anau 9600 •* www.barnyardbackpackers.com

---

Tourist information

While there is no tourism information center, the Real Journeys office is always happy to help.

South Island's lower east coast

Dunedin

Dunedin Railway Station

Dunedin is a large city surrounded by dramatic hills and full of Victorian and Edwardian architecture. Rich in Scottish heritage, it's known as the Edinburgh of New Zealand. These days it's a big university city, with a young and vibrant population attracting a good number of cheap places to stay or eat out in. It's recommended to spend at least an afternoon or morning here to soak it all in before heading off on your journeys.

Things to do

To get your bearings, first head to the Octagon, the circular street in the city center. Most spots are a short walk, quick drive or short bus ride away.

Otago Museum

Comprising more than a million objects, this museum does an excellent job at telling visitors about the history, nature and culture of Dunedin and the surrounding Otago region. There's lots on the Maori people in particular, with an impressive collection of treasures, and a huge selection of articulated moa skeletons. *FREE • 10am-5pm •* www.otagomuseum.nz *• 10-15 minute walk from the city center, up State Highway 1, passing Dunedin Hospital*

Walk up Baldwin Street

New Zealanders like to say this is the steepest residential street in the world, and after hiking up it we can see why! Along the way visitors can get some rather amusing pictures alongside the funnily-angled trees and homes. *Just put Baldwin Street into your GPS or take bus route 8 in the direction of Normandy and get off at 275 North Road*

Explore the city's street graffiti

The city of Dunedin actively encourages artists to create street art, even bringing artists from across the world to create pieces on Dunedin's walls. These are everywhere, and you're sure to come across some amazing ones as you just walk around, but if you have some free time and want to explore more check out the current map of art work at http://dunedinstreetart.co.nz/artworks.

Dunedin Railway Station

Even if you're not doing a train ride on the Taieri Gorge, visitors to Dunedin should have a look inside this Renaissance-style building. Built way back in 1906, it features a lavish interior with a booking hall that has about 750,000 tiles of Royal Doulton porcelain. The outside is just as grand, and certainly requires a picture for Instagram or Facebook!

Budget food

George Street, heading north from the Octagon, is the best place to head for a cheap meal out. It's all here, from budget kebab joints to Asian food and fish and chips. A local favorite is Chopsticks 101, near ASB bank, which offers large portions of Chinese food for not too bad a price (11:30am-9pm, meals from $12). Having said that, as the hostels in town have great kitchens and there are a few huge supermarkets in the city center, most budget travelers should self-cater in Dunedin.

Cheap supermarkets

In the city center, there's a Countdown supermarket a short walk west of the Octagon (6am-11pm), as well as a New World a few minutes north on Great King Street (7:20am-10pm).

Recommended cheap accommodation

On Top Backpackers

It's not exactly The Ritz, but there is a free breakfast and it's a great place to meet fellow travelers at the bar downstairs and the comfy lounge. *Beds from $26 • Tel: 03 477 6121 • 12 Filleul Street, 9016 Dunedin •* https://on-top-backpackers-nz.book.direct

Manor House Backpackers

Friendly hostel with both dorm and private rooms, free wifi and a spacious kitchen. All you need for a good night's sleep then! *Beds from $35 • Tel: 03 477 0484 • 28 Manor Place, Dunedin, 9016 •* https://thebackpackergroup.co.nz/our-hostels/manor-house

How to get there and away

By bus

Kiwi Experience can drop you off in Dunedin if you get the right bus pass. Alternatively, InterCity can take you all over the South Island from here, such as to Christchurch (6 hours, around $55-65), Te Anau (5 hours, around $50) and Queenstown (5 hours, around $50).

By car or campervan

Dunedin is three hours north from Invercargill and about one hour from Moeraki via State Highway 1. Check road conditions before as roads can be closed at times.

By air

Budget airline Jetstar has flights here, as well as Air New Zealand and Virgin Australia. Super Shuttle (www.supershuttle.co.nz) provides a shuttle service from the city (1 hour, $20).

Free Wifi

There is free wifi in the Octagon, as well as the museum and railway station.

Tourist information

The main i-SITE is located at the Octagon, in the city center (8:30am-5pm).

Dunedin to Queenstown via the Taieri Gorge

Stopping for a short break at the teeny-tiny Hindon station on The Taieri Gorge Railway

Many years ago there used to be a railway that went all the way from Dunedin to Cromwell, near Queenstown. Sadly closed decades ago due to low ridership, the route has since been revitalized with a tourist train and cycling tracks. Along the way, you'll pass over grand railway bridges, through old tunnels, past abandoned gold diggings and see plenty of classic Art Deco architecture and plenty of rustic farms. It's all very New Zealand!

First, the Taieri Gorge Railway takes riders from Dunedin's Victorian station to Pukerangi (or nearby Middlemarch occasionally) via this highly scenic gorge. From Pukerangi, you can take a shuttle bus to Middlemarch to pick up your bike, or start from here if you have your own. Travelers can then continue on their bikes along the mostly flat route that the railway used to take, a relaxing ride that is suitable for almost all ages. The 150km cycling route usually takes 1-5 days, depending on your fitness level.

Step 1) Take the Taieri Gorge Railway to Pukerangi

Trains take about two hours and run once or twice a day from Dunedin station to Pukerangi. Make sure you plan and book early, as some days might not have departures and prices can vary significantly, especially in summer. Bikes can be transported on the trains. Book online at www.dunedinrailways.co.nz. *Adults from around $60, children from $20*

Step 2) Cycle from Middlemarch to Clyde on the Otago Central Rail Trail

Pick up a bike from one of the hire companies in town if you need to, then head to the starting post at Middlemarch station. The route is well signposted, with maps and informative displays in the old station buildings (just old metal huts in some cases!) helping to bring the old railway's story to life.

Three days and two nights should be enough for the average person to do the whole route, which would mean about five or six hours each day cycling. Staying at the recommended accommodations in Ranfurly and Ophir would be a good plan for such people. Some people cut the length of the cycle ride by getting one of the shuttle bus companies to drop them off somewhere along the route. Another alternative is to stay an extra night or two to break up the journey.

Spectacular views along the Otago Central Rail Trail

Step 3) Bus or hitchhike to Queenstown

InterCity, as well as the shuttle bus companies, have a few buses a day that can take you from Clyde or the nearby Alexandra to Queenstown or other locations in the South Island. If bringing your own bike on InterCity, you just need to give $10 in cash to the driver as this will be classed as oversized baggage. A lot of people will also be heading west to Queenstown as well, so hitchhiking shouldn't be too difficult.

Bike rental and shuttle bus companies

There are a few companies to choose from, with varying prices and options:

Cycle Surgery
Amid a wide selection of shuttle bus and bike hire options, we used Cycle Surgery and found their bikes to be very reliable and shuttle buses were always on time. *Adult bikes from $40 a day, children's bikes from $30 a day. Pukerangi to Middlemarch shuttle bus $30* • www.cyclesurgery.co.nz

Trail Journeys
This reputable company offers shuttles buses and bike hires, as well as plenty of guided tours, luggage services, a door-to-door bus service from Dunedin and lots more. *Adult bikes from $50 a day, children's bikes from $27 a day. Pukerangi to Middlemarch shuttle bus $25* • www.cyclesurgery.co.nz

She Bikes She Bikes

This up-and-coming bike hire company has some excellent mountain bikes and e-bikes. *Adult bikes from $45 a day, children's bikes from $30 a day* • shebikeshebikes.co.nz

Budget food

Along the way there are Four Square supermarkets in Omakau (7:30am-7pm), Ranfurly (7am-6pm) and Alexandra (7am-10pm), as well as the odd general store. These are easy to find as most villages are pretty small. There are long stretches of the trail that won't have any shops to buy drinks, so come prepared. Note that many places do not open in winter, so you may need to bring food with you if you can't find accommodation that provides it.

There are some slightly pricey cafes and pubs along the way, but here are the best bets for budget travelers looking to eat in or get a takeaway along the way:

Balmoral Dairy & Takeaway - Fish and chips, plus Chinese food available. Also has a small convenience store section. *Meals $8-10, snacks $4-$7 • 9:30am-8:30pm (closed Mondays) • In Ranfurly, a few minutes north up the main road from the Challenge gas station*

Maniototo Cafe - Pleasant cafe with supermarket next door. *Light meals $5-10 • 7am-4:30pm (until 5pm on weekends) • Outside Ranfurly station*

Muddy Creek Cafe & Takeaway - Excellent fish and chip joint. Also has super tasty pies! *Meals from $7-10 • 8:30am-7pm • In Omakau, opposite the gas station*

Recommended cheap accommodation

An official list of accommodations drawn up by the Otago Central Rail Trail Charitable Trust is at www.otagocentralrailtrail.co.nz/where-to-stay/. Please note that many of the accommodations do not open in winter. Here are the best places along the cycling trail for those on a budget:

Old Post Office Backpackers

Well-maintained rooms with an excellent, knowledgeable owner and a comfy lounge to chill out in. *Dorm beds $35, private rooms from $60 • Tel: 03 444 9588 • 11 Pery Street, Ranfurly, Central Otago, 9332* • www.oldpobackpackers.co.nz

Crows Nest

At about the halfway point, this cozy place is a great option if you want to give yourself three nights, or you want to smash it in one night and two days! *Tent sites $15, dorm beds $30, private rooms from $115 • Tel: 03 444 5063 • 3365 Ida Valley-Omakau Road, Oturehua, Central Otago, 9389* • https://crowsnestcentralotago.wordpress.com

Ophir Lodge

Lovely little huts are on offer here, with a big kitchen, lounge and free breakfast buffet to stuff yourself on in the morning. *Beds from $37 • Tel: 022 6437 781 • 1 Macdonald Street, Ophir, Central Otago, 9393* • http://ophirlodge.co.nz

Tourist information

Ranfurly has an i-SITE in the station building (9am-5:30pm), while Alexandra has one in Pioneer Park along the main shopping street on State Highway 8 (9am-6pm).

Oamaru

Oamaru is a town rich in history and a very worthwhile stop-off as you head up the east coast. Featuring some of the country's oldest surviving buildings, it does feel like you're back in the 19th century at points. The town is very proud of its heritage, and the quirky locals love to show it off in all kinds of ways. The steampunk craze is a great example of this, which can be seen as you walk around town as well as a museum. There are also penguin colonies.

Things to do

Oamaru Victorian Heritage Precinct

A very picturesque street lined with well-preserved heritage buildings from the Victorian era. The precinct has a host of art galleries, shops and craft shops to explore, often inspired by the good old times. While these tend to be a little pricey, the area is a perfect place for a free stroll and a bit of photo taking. *Short walk from main road. Location is well signposted*

Steampunk HQ

A very unique, quirky museum set in a grain elevator building from the 1880s. Based on the heritage precinct, it's full of funny displays, art pieces and light shows that illustrate the dream of an industrial, steampunk world. *$10 • 10am-5pm •* www.steampunkoamaru.co.nz *• On the way to the heritage precinct, near the tourist information center*

Steampunk Playground

If you don't want to spend money on Steampunk HQ, just head down to this garden and playground instead to see some rather cool steampunk creations. It's also a great place to take the little ones of course! *FREE • 24h • Down the end of the Victorian Heritage Precinct*

See the Blue Penguins

Penguins began to settle in the rock quarry in the early 1990s, and since then it's become one of Oamaru's most popular things to do. During the day visitors can enter the viewing rooms and breeding area, but the best time to come is in the evening. This is when you'll be able to see the penguins arrive home from fishing for the day, to the safety of the rocks. The easiest way to do this is to enter the paid-for seating area, but some people get lucky by just finding a seat on the waterfront nearby. *From $18 in the day, $32 in the evening • On the day you're visiting, check* www.penguins.co.nz *for the best time to see the penguins • Several minutes on foot down the waterfront from the heritage precinct*

Discount stores

Discount variety megastore The Warehouse is a short walk up Thames Street from the i-SITE Visitor Information Centre, next to the Countdown supermarket (8am-8pm).

Budget food

It's mostly expensive around the Oamaru Victorian Heritage Precinct, but there are some cheap places north of here. Head up Thames Street, and past the Countdown supermarket and there are some cheap Chinese, Indian, Thai and fast food restaurants. For something more interesting, Asta la Pasta make super delicious fresh pasta takeaways (from $10, irregular hours), so check out their Facebook page (www.facebook.com/astalapastaoamaru) for their current whereabouts if you are interested.

Cheap supermarkets

There is a Countdown supermarket about five minutes up Thames Street from the visitor center (7am-9pm), so self-catering is a great idea here if you are staying in town.

Recommended cheap accommodation

Swaggers Backpackers

Really friendly backpackers with a 'Camp Mum' called Agra, a lady who always has a smile on her face and loves to help travelers to get around Oamaru. *Private rooms from $80, dorms from $30 • Tel: 03 434 9999 • 25 Wansbeck Street, Oamaru •* www.swaggersbackpackers.co.nz

YHA Oamaru

A short walk from the town center and the penguins, this small YHA has a BBQ and well-equipped kitchen. *Private rooms from $66, dorms from $30 • Tel: 03 434 5008 • 2 Reed Street, Oamaru •* www.yha.co.nz

Empire Hotel Backpackers (BBH)

Two lounges to relax in on the evenings, with a pool table, a piano and much more. You can see why this hostel is a favorite with many backpackers. *Beds from $30 (from $26 with BBH card) • Tel: 03 434 3446 • 13 Thames Street, Oamaru •* www.empirebackpackersoamaru.co.nz

---

How to get there and away

By bus

Atomic Travel stops off in Oamaru on route from Dunedin (2 hours, $20) to Christchurch (4 hours, $35). InterCity also has coaches from Christchurch (4 hours, from $36) and Dunedin (2 hours, $16-$32), as well as connections to many other locations in the South Island.

By car or campervan

Oamaru is half an hour from Moeraki and Elephant Rocks. It's also one hour from Dunedin and three hours from Christchurch via State Highway 1.

Tourist information

The i-SITE Visitor Information Centre is near the Steampunk HQ (9am-5pm).

Elephant Rocks

An interesting place to stop off at if you have your own vehicle, the Elephant Rocks are a collection of towering limestone rocks scattered over a quiet hillside. Varying from one to ten meters tall, they are considered to be a geological wonder of the Waitaki and have been featured in movies such as The Lion, the Witch and the Wardrobe. *FREE • 24h • Head towards a town called Duntroon on State Highway 83 from Oamaru (40 mins), or Omarama (1 hour). As you approach Duntroon, follow signs to the Elephant Rocks, which is on Island Cliff-Duntroon Road*

Moeraki Boulders

A popular spot to stop off at if you are heading down the stunning coast on State Highway 1, the Moeraki Boulders are a group of more than 50 huge spherical stones located on a pristine beach. Formed over millions of years, the boulders are often more than two meters wide, and are believed to have formed as the waves eroded the soft mudstone surrounding the boulders, releasing them onto the beach. Early morning or late afternoon is usually best, but check for low tides with the Met Service at www.metservice.com/marine/surf/moeraki if you want to be sure. *FREE • 24h • By car: head towards Hampden on State Highway 1 from Dunedin (1 hour) or Oamaru (30 mins). The boulders are on Koekohe Beach, a few minutes south of Hampden. By bus: InterCity can also drop you off at Hampden or the Moeraki Turn Off*

Stewart Island (Rakiura)

New Zealand's third biggest island, Stewart Island is a hotspot for seeing kiwi and other birdlife, as well as for hiking, with trails for both short walks and multi-day excursions. The only settlement on the island is a town called Oban, with the rest of the island being reserved as a national park. The only 400 or so locals are a friendly bunch of people, but are actually outnumbered by brown kiwi and Tokoeka birds. Visitors will also have a chance to see blue penguins and seals on their trip.

Things to do

Rakiura Museum

Learn about the island's history and get a preview of what you'll see on your hikes at this lovely little museum. Staff are very knowledgeable and passionate about the island area, and have created some fascinating displays and mini exhibitions. *FREE • 10am-1:30pm •* www.rakiuramuseum.co.nz *• Located on Main Street*

See the kiwi

By far the best experience on Stewart Island if you're lucky enough to see the little creatures that New Zealanders are named after. While it's apparently possible to see them around the rugby field in Oban, your chances of seeing them are far better if you join a tour with a guide who knows exactly how and where to find them:

Evening Eco Watch / Kiwi Spotting

This tour takes you in a small group around the walking tracks surrounding Oban in search of the kiwi. After an informative talk by one of the local kiwi experts, plus a Q&A session, you'll set off on a mini-bus to various short walks in areas where the elusive birds may be located. Tour price includes transportation back to your accommodation. *Adults $135, children $95 • Operates when enough people want to join (always book in advance) •* www.ruggedyrange.com *• Departs from the Ruggedy Range office, near the Department of Conservation office*

Wild Kiwi Encounter

For those that want the ultimate kiwi experience and the best chance of seeing them. After taking a cruise around the coves and smaller islands dotting the area, passengers are taken to a small wharf called The Neck. From here they are led by a nature guide through the forest, via a secluded beach, on the search for kiwi. No need to bring drinks, as there is free tea and coffee on board the boats. Prices are quite steep, so check what deals are currently on offer at www.stewartislandexperience.co.nz/plan-your-trip/specials. *$199 (adults only) • Evenings September to mid-May • www.stewartislandexperience.co.nz • Departs from the same ferry terminal in Oban as the Bluff ferry*

Visit Ulva Island

Ulva Island is a wildlife sanctuary, full of colorful birdlife and all sorts of weird and wonderful plant life. There are a variety of walking courses around the small island, all mainly on flat land and well signposted with maps. There are a few ways to get there:

Ulva Island Ferry

The best way to do Ulva Island for most budget travelers, as once you get to the island, it's super easy to get around and you'll see all the same nature and plants as those on a guided tour. *Adults $20, children $10 • Departs Golden Bay: 9am, 12pm, 2pm, 4pm. Returns from Ulva Island: 12.15pm, 2.15pm, 4.15pm (closed in winter) • www.stewartisland.co.nz/organisations/water-taxi/ulva-island-ferry/ • Departs from Golden Bay, a 15 minute walk to the southwest of Oban*

Cruise and tour with Stewart Island Experience

If you are particularly interested in the nature and want a nature guide to explain it all and answer any questions you might have, then join a tour to Ulva Island with Stewart Island Experience. The two-and-a-half-hour package includes a cruise around the nearby coves and deserted beaches, plus a 45-minute guided walk. *Adults $99, children $30 • Usually 12pm (September to May) • www.stewartislandexperience.co.nz • Departs from the same ferry terminal in Oban as the Bluff ferry*

Hikes and walks around Stewart Island

There are numerous hiking and walking tracks on Stewart Island, from a quick 10-minute stroll along the beach to multi-day hikes. Head to the Department of Conservation office for a free map and track updates, which will probably be necessary for most routes. Below are some of the best for budget travelers starting from Oban, but if you're looking for something more challenging head to www.stewartisland.co.nz/walks for a full list of hikes.

Observation Rock

Most visitors to the island take the steep walk up to Observation Rock for views of the stunning Paterson Inlet. It's especially beautiful at sunrise or sunset. *Difficulty: Easy • Time required: 30 minutes • Head down Ayr Street from the waterfront and follow signs*

Golden Bay-Deep Bay Walk

Providing panoramic views of Ulva Island and Halfmoon Bay from up Peterson Hill, this winding track through nearby forest is a good option most times of the year, even if it's raining a bit. *Difficulty: Medium • Time required: 2 hours return • Trail starts from the waterfront*

Fuchsia and Raroa Reserve Walk

A protected area of lush natural forest, in summer alive with the sound of bellbirds and wood pigeons. It's been untouched by past milling operations that effected other areas on the island, meaning you'll be walking through habitats rich in native fern, moss and other vibrant plant life. There are two tracks on offer, and these can be combined with a hike up Observation Rock. *Difficulty: Medium • Time required: 1 hour • Walk up Ayr Road from the waterfront, then head down Dundee Street and follow the signs*

Budget food

Just Cafe - Cozy little place, with a range of freshly made sandwiches and cakes, plus ice cream for the summer. *Light meals $6-12 • Opening time vary • Up Main Street, near Four Square supermarket*
Kai Kart - Fish and chips, as well as some very hearty burgers. The hut looks rather unassuming, but the meals really hit the spot. *Meals $10-15 • 10am-1:30pm • Near Rakiura Museum on Ayr Street*

Cheap supermarkets

Surprisingly for a settlement as small as Oban there is a medium-sized Four Square supermarket, which is located on the bay (7:30am-7pm).

Recommended cheap accommodation

Apart from the below two backpackers and camping, other accommodation in town is usually prohibitively expensive, so book as early as you can.

Stewart Island Backpackers
Tent sites, dorm beds and all sorts of private rooms are on offer at this hostel. There is a decent lounge with a pool table and games to play, which is great as there is not much of a night life in Oban. *Beds from $36, tent sites $23 • Tel: 03 219 1114 • 18 Ayr Street, Stewart Island, 9818* • www.stewartislandbackpackers.co.nz

Bunkers Backpackers
Centrally located, with an outside BBQ area to cook all that cheap meat and veggies from Four Square! Friendly atmosphere, with a comfortable lounge and well-equipped kitchen. *Beds from $36 • Tel: 027 738 1796 • 13 Argyle Street, Halfmoon Bay* • www.bunkersbackpackers.co.nz

How to get there and away

By ferry

Real Journeys, via their subsidiary Stewart Island Experience, provide an excellent service on their speedy catamarans from a town called Bluff (1 hour, adults $148, children $74 return), plus there is complimentary tea and coffee on board! Especially during busy times, it's highly recommended to pre-book at www.stewartislandexperience.co.nz to avoid any disappointment. There is ample parking outside their Bluff ferry terminal for those who want to park their cars while in Stewart Island.

Real Journeys also offer coach and ferry packages from Queenstown (4 hours, adults $266, children $133 return), Te Anau (5 hours, $266, children $133 return) and Invercargill (1 hour, adults $200, children $100 return) on a seasonal basis.

Additionally, Tracknet (https://tracknet.net) provides transportation from Bluff and Invercargill to other towns in the south, while Catch-A-Bus South provide a slightly more expensive service for those who require a door-to-door service.

By air

Stewart Island Flights (www.stewartislandflights.co.nz) provide a regular service to and from the island, but with prices starting from $130 one-way, it's not really for budget travelers. Flights depart from Invercargill on the mainland.

Tourist information

There is a Department of Conservation office on Main Road (8:30am-4:30pm), while the Oban Visitor Centre is located a minute down the road after you get off the ferry (8am-6pm).

South Island's west coast

Fox Glacier

Descending from the Southern Alps down into the forests below, Fox Glacier is one of the most accessible glaciers in the country. While It's not as impressive as Franz Josef, it's still many kilometers long and a quick extra excursion as you make your way up or down the west coast. There is also a nearby village where you can get some supplies or enjoy a meal.

The easiest way to get a view of the glacier is to take the Fox Glacier Valley Walk, from which it takes a matter of minutes before you start to see the glacier. You'll cross several small creeks and streams, before a steep climb to the viewing area where you'll be able to get reasonably close to the glacier. The ice is always on the move, so you may see ice or rocks falling and water levels can change at a moment's notice. Make sure you observe all warning signs to stay safe! If you're staying in town you can also walk or cycle to the car park where the trail starts, via the Te Weheka Walkway and Minnehaha Walk, which add about two hours to the return trip on foot or one hour by bicycle. *Difficulty: Easy • Time required: 1 hour return • Starts from the car park. Follow signs to the carpark as you approach on State Highway 6 if driving here •* www.glaciercountry.co.nz *(use this website to check glacier is accessible before going)*

Budget food

It's mostly expensive cafes and bars here, but there are always bargains to be had and all the restaurants are near to each other. The following are in order from south to north along State Highway 6:

Fox Glacier Guiding Cafe (Hobnail Cafe) - All sorts of healthy sandwiches and vegetarian snacks are available, as well as fancy lunches. *Meals $12-16, snacks $4-6 • 7:30am-4:30pm • Next to the Glacier Tours booking office*

Cafe Neve - Cozy coffee spot, which also sells pies, milkshakes and sandwiches for takeout. *Light meals from $6 • 8am-5pm • Next to the general store*

Cook Saddle Cafe & Saloon - The takeout menu here has some perfectly reasonable prices, with a healthy selection of battered and deep-fried meals available. *Takeout items from $3 • 8am-3pm • Next to the Glacier Helicopters Fox Glacier office on State Highway 6*

Cheap supermarkets

The Fox Glacier General Store, in the town center on State Highway 6, has a small selection of basics (8am-8pm), but Four Square up the road in Franz Josef is a lot larger and has better prices (7:45am-7:30pm). The gas station also has a small shop.

Recommended cheap accommodation

Ivory Towers Backpackers

This long-established hostel, located in the center of town, offers amazing views from its balconies, a comfortable lounge and a large collection of movies to watch in the evening. All sorts of rooms are available, from dorms to family cottages. *Private rooms from $56, dorms from $26 • Tel: 03 751 0838 • 33/35 Sullivans Road, Fox Glacier 3281 •* https://ivorytowers.co.nz

Fox Glacier Pod Hostel & Inn

This might be a better choice if you want to pay hostel prices but need your own space. Guests stay in little pods, but standard private rooms are also on offer. There is free soup in the evening, as well as free popcorn on occasion! *Beds from $25 • Tel: 03 751 0022 • 39 Sullivan Road, Fox Glacier 7886 •* https://foxglacierinn.co.nz

---

How to get there and away

By bus

InterCity operate a coach line up the west coast, with buses from places like Queenstown (6 hours, $69), Wanaka (5 hours, $55), Greymouth (4 hours, $47) and Franz Josef (30 minutes, $28). Both Kiwi Experience and Stray can drop off customers using their bus passes.

By car or campervan

Fox Glacier is one hour and a half from Haast and three and a half hours from Wanaka via State Highway 6. Heading north it's only 20 minutes from Franz Josef and then another two hours to Greymouth. There is a gas station in the town center.

Tourist information

The nearest official tourist information center, i-SITE, is in Franz Josef (9am-5pm), but local tour operators have offices in the town of Fox Glacier if you need help. Try to avoid fake information centers who actually just want to sell you expensive tours and are not interested in offering general guidance, which some tourists have reported coming across.

Stop-off point: Haast

Haast is a tiny community about halfway from Wanaka to Fox Glacier, and so is an excellent place to stop for food or to stretch your legs. Just make a turn into the settlement as you approach from State Highway 6, and the following spots are easy to find. There is also a gas station.

Otoko Espresso - Cute little mobile coffee joint. Has snacks using local ingredients, such as whitebait fritters and venison. There is also sometimes a fish and chips truck parked nearby. *Drinks and snacks $4-5 • 8:30am-5pm (until 4pm in winter) • Halfway down Marks Road*

Grumpy Cow - English breakfasts, burgers and hotdogs, plus tasty toasties. They also have a decent supermarket attached. *Eat-in meals $8-16, takeaways snacks from $0.80 • 9am-7pm • On Pauareka Road*

Franz Josef (Waiau)

Franz Josef is a World Heritage-listed glacier, and in many opinions the most interesting one to visit in New Zealand. Larger than the nearby Fox Glacier, Franz Josef Glacier has many walking, hiking and cycling tracks from which visitors can immerse themselves in the nearby rainforests and also see the glacier itself. The town of the same name is reasonably well built for those on a budget, with a supermarket, a few cheap places to eat and hostels with excellent rates.

Things to do

Local churches

The historic St James Anglican Church to the south end of the town was built in the 1930s, at a time when you could see the glacier from the church windows! During times when a service is not on, visitors can have a peek inside and also explore the lovely little church grounds. Down the road is also the Catholic church, Our Lady Of The Alps, a modest church with stained-glass windows. Read the historic information boards for a quick insight into the lives of the early British settlers.

Activities and tours

If you have more than a day here, there are a few fun activities that you can participate in. Don't forget to check for any deals at www.bookme.co.nz before you reserve anything, as prices here are generally higher than at many other tourist towns.

Glacier Hot Pools

OK, so maybe it's not exactly the cheapest way to spend an hour or two, but chilling out in these hot pools might be necessary after an exhausting hike! *Adults $28, children $24 • 11am-9pm* • www.glacierhotpools.co.nz

Across Country Quad Bikes

Do something a little different, and have a go on an ATV quad bike through the nearby rivers, forest and grassland. It's an exhilarating experience, and definitely one for daredevils. All the necessary gear is provided. Check the official website for combo deals. *$70-$160 • Various times throughout the day •* www.acrosscountryquadbikes.co.nz

Skydive Franz Josef Glacier

Claiming to be New Zealand's highest skydive at an amazing 20,000ft, Skydive Franz Josef Glacier will drop you off among some of the country's highest mountains and biggest glaciers, as well as within view of the ocean to the west. *Skydives from $319 • Various time slots from 8am-6pm •* www.skydivefranz.co.nz

Map of Franz Josef Village

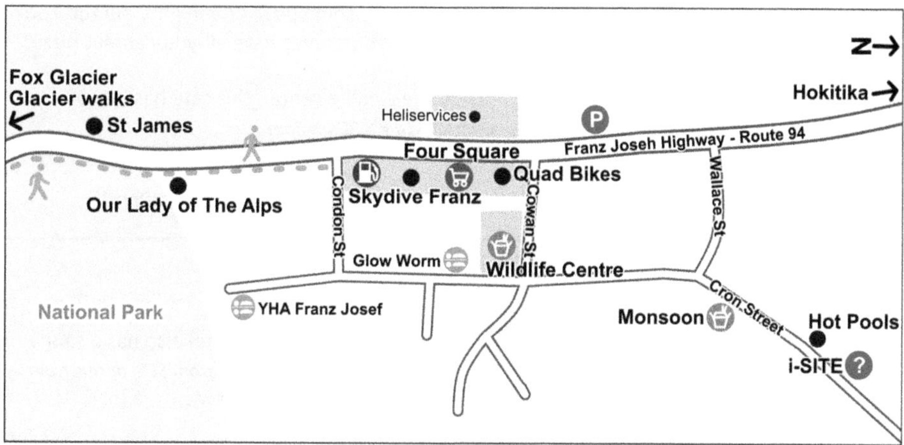

Hikes and walks

Here are the main walks to do around the glacier:

Glacier Valley Walk

Starting with the Forest Walk, an easy trail along the glacial river that leads from Franz Josef, walkers follow a series of markers up to the 'terminal face' of the glacier. You'll be walking over small rocks and around the riverbed, so bring good footwear as it's a bit rough at points. It's worth it in the end though, when you see the magnificent glacier! *Difficulty: Easy • Time required: around 2 hours return • Starts from main car park*

Te Ara a Waiau Walkway/Cycleway

A convenient way to get to the glacier and nearby walks from town, so perfect if you don't have a vehicle or want more of a challenge. This path follows the glacier valley access road, occasionally veering off into the unspoiled forest. *Difficulty: Easy • Time required: 2 hours return on foot, 1 hour return via bicycle • Head south past the Catholic church, then cross the river. The track then runs up the glacier access road until it reaches the car parks*

Peters Pool Walk

A pleasant addition or add-on to your day of hiking if you have time after seeing the glacier. This track winds through the rainforest before coming to Peters Pool, a lake formed by melting ice more than 200 years ago. When the weather is nice, the lake provides a stunning reflective view of the mountains and glacier. *Difficulty: Easy • Time required: 20-25 minutes • Starts from the main car park or from the end of Douglas Walk*

Douglas Walk

Another non-strenuous forest walk, this one crosses various glacial landform, giving walkers an insight into the various stages of regrowth as the ice moved through this area thousands of years ago. Definitely less busy than many other walks. This path continues on from the Peters Pool Walk, and afterwards you can return to the main car park via the Te Ara a Waiau Walkway. *Difficulty: Easy • Time required: around 1 hour • Starts from the main car park, via the Peter Pool Walk, or at the smaller car park to the north*

Budget food

Most budget travelers will cook their own food back at their hostel in Franz Josef, but there are a few places that aren't too expensive:

Monsoon Restaurant - Sit around the fireplace and enjoy some pizza or a mighty burger. Look out for the cheap backpacker meals for $12. They also sometimes have all-you-can-eat pizza. *Meals $12-20 • 4:30pm-1am*

West Coast Wildlife Centre - Located right inside the wildlife center, this cafe has lots of homemade pies, sandwiches and quiches. *Meals $8-14 • 8:30am-8pm*

Cheap supermarkets

Four Square has a moderately sized supermarket on the main road (7:45am-7:30pm).

Recommended cheap accommodation

YHA Franz Josef

As well as the standard YHA fare of free wifi and a comfy lounge, this hostel also has a sauna and a pretty sweet view of the rainforest from most rooms. *Private rooms from $60, dorms from $22 (10% off for YHA members) • Tel: 03 752 0754 • 2-4 Cron Street, Franz Josef •* www.yha.co.nz

Glow Worm Accommodation

This hostel also has both dorms and private rooms. Additionally it has free unlimited wifi, free breakfasts and evening soups for all guests, plus free popcorn too! *Private rooms from $70, dorms from $28 • Tel: 0800 151 027 • 27 Cron Street, Franz Josef Glacier •* www.glowwormfranz.co.nz

---

How to get there and away

By bus

The InterCity buses going up the west coast all stop here, with direct buses from Queenstown (7-8 hours, $73), Greymouth (4 hours, $44) and Fox Glacier (30 minutes, $28). Both Kiwi Experience and Stray buses also stop here.

By car or campervan

The town of Franz Josef is 20 minutes north of Fox Glacier and just over two hours from Greymouth on highway State Highway 6. It's about three hours from Arthur's Pass.

Tourist information

The Franz Josef i-SITE Visitor Information Centre is located down Cron Street (9am-5pm).

Hokitika

View through the native forest towards Lake Mahinapua

Hokitika is a small town that most travelers should visit as they head along the west coast. Along with the first supermarket in a long time, Hokitika is also the only major town on the coast with a beach. It's an excellent place to stretch your legs, enjoy a casual stroll and take a photo or two, especially during the vivid sunsets.

Things to do

See the Pounamu artists

The town is also known as the birthplace of pounamu, or greenstone, that you'll see in all the gift shops on the South Island. As you walk around the town center, you'll come across free galleries displaying local artists' work with pounamu, as well as a chance to observe them making their pieces.

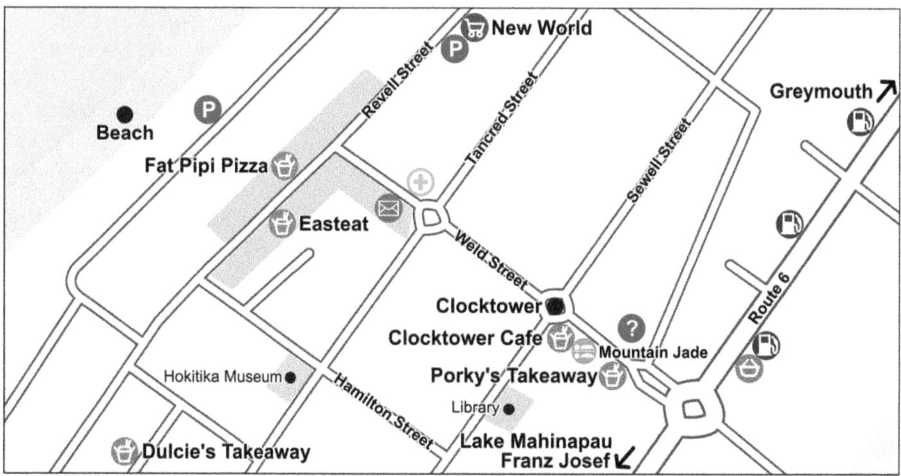

Lake Mahinapua

A tranquil lake just south of Hokitika, Lake Mahinapua is surrounded by native bush, with the central Alps mountains in the distance. It's a convenient, and pretty place to stop off for a picnic or drink, plus the water is usually warm enough for a quick swim! You can also take a walk on one of the many easy tracks around and nearby the lake. All in all a must visit if you are driving up the west coast. *The lake is 10 minutes south of Hokitika by car. Just head down State Highway 6 and follow signs to Lake Mahinapua. Kiwi Experience can also take you here on their buses*

Budget food

The town is full of cheap cafes, fish and chip takeaways, and ice cream shops. Here are some highlights (see town map for locations):
Porky's Takeaways - Large selection of fish, chips, burgers and deep-fried desserts. *Meals $6-10 • 11am-8:30pm*
Clocktower Cafe - Hearty, big sandwiches, handmade pies and all day breakfasts. Also a convenient place to try whitebait, a west coast delicacy. *Meals $8-12 • 6:30am-4pm*
Easteat Restaurant - Decent portions of Chinese food using local ingredients. Everything from fried rice to lemon chicken. *Meals from $12 • 11am-9pm*
Fat Pipi Pizza - Try some tasty pizzas with somewhat crazy, yet imaginative toppings. Probably a perfect place to go if you are fed up eating deep-fried food. *Meal deals $10-20 • 12pm-2:30pm, 5pm-8pm (until 9pm on Fridays and Saturdays)*
Dulcie's Takeaways - Well regarded fish and chip joint. Also has some pretty gorgeous chocolate filled donuts. *Meals $6-10 • 11am-7:30pm*

Cheap supermarkets

There is a New World supermarket in the town center, on Revell Street (8am-9pm).

Recommended cheap accommodation

Mountain Jade Backpackers (BBH)
Various discounts are available, especially for multi-day stays. Also includes free breakfast. *Beds from $26 for BBH members, from $30 for non-members • Tel: 03 755 5185 • 41 Weld Street, Hokitika •* www.mountainjadebackpackers.co.nz

YHA Hokitika
Spacious hostel with lots of charm and great ocean views. This hostel is a short drive from town, so best for those with their own vehicle. *Private rooms from $98, dorms from $37 • Tel: 03 755 7179 • 124 Kumara Junction Highway, Two Mile, Hokitika •* www.yha.co.nz

---

How to get there and away

By bus

Kiwi Experience takes people to Lake Mahinapua on some of their passes. InterCity's west coast route also stops off in Hokitika, but it might be a bit pointless to stop here rather than more interesting spots like Arthur's Pass or Franz Josef.

By car or campervan

Hokitika is nearly two hours from Franz Josef up State Highway 6, and one hour from Arthur's Pass. Road signs make it easy to find your way.

Tourist information

The i-SITE (8:30am-5pm) is just off State Highway 6. Follow signs as you head into the town.

Stop-off point: Greymouth

Greymouth is a reasonably large town, and probably the biggest on the west coast. If you are on a bus or train, there is not too much to do here other than grab a meal or get a night's sleep if you're arriving late. There are also a few gas stations along the main road if you need to refill. Below are some places that you may want or need to pop into, but there are also some cool little cafes, bakeries and more in the town center if you have time to explore.

Countdown - Large supermarket with parking available. *7am-9pm • Follow signs to the train station. Countdown is just behind it*

The Warehouse - Head in here if you need to get any bulk food items or travel products on the cheap. Also has free parking. *7am-9pm • Next to Countdown*

Subway - Branch of the international sandwich chain, with daily deals to help keep your food costs down. *Sandwiches from $5 • 7am-9pm • Just around the corner from The Warehouse*

Arthur's Pass

Hiking up the hills and mountains of Arthur's Pass

Arthur's Pass is a small village about halfway between Christchurch and Greymouth, nestled in the heart of the Southern Alps. It's a very quiet settlement, with not much development having taken place, and only basic facilities available. It therefore doesn't feel touristy at all, and quite an authentic New Zealand experience.

Arthur's Pass offers a wealth of spectacular walking and hiking opportunities in the surrounding national park. Even if you're not much of a hiker, this is the most scenic way to cross from Christchurch to the west coast.

Things to do

Arthur's Pass National Park is another place where you might come across the rather naughty kea, a kind of alpine parrot that loves to grab people's food! The park itself has a diverse range of habitats, with the eastern part being full of beech forest and shingle-filled riverbeds, while the western side has many deep rivers and dense rainforest.

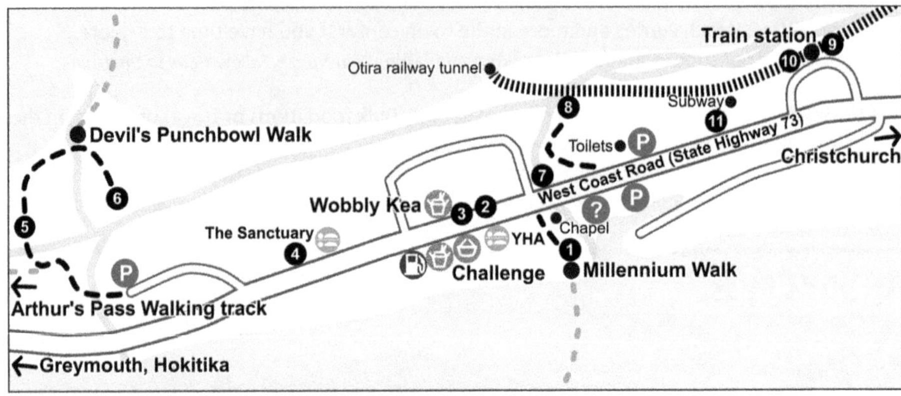

Walks starting from the village or nearby

Devil's Punchbowl

While it's possible to see the waterfall through the trees as you head down State Highway 73, anyone visiting Arthur's Pass should make the walk up to the base of the waterfall. After heading through the native forest, Punchbowl Creek and over a few footbridges, walkers then head up a steep set of steps to a viewing platform for the magnificent 131-meter high waterfall. *Difficulty: Easy • Time required: 1 hour return • Heading north from the village, go down Punchbowl Road and follow the green signs to the track*

Arthur's Pass Historic Walk

The village is dotted with information boards that provide a look back at what Arthur's Pass was like in the early 1900s. It's an easy walk around the village to the various places of interest. *Difficulty: Very easy • Time required: 1-2 hours, but can be done in parts • See map for locations (numbered icons), or just explore the town on your own and you'll come across many of them*

Millennium Walk

This leisurely walk would be a good bet if you have children or aren't much of a walker. The route starts with a walk over a cute little stone bridge, then continues to a viewing platform for the nearby waterfall. *Difficulty: Easy • Time required: 10 minutes • Starts from the visitor center*

Arthur's Pass Walking Track

Another classic walk to do here, this new trail links a series of old tracks. Along the way you'll not just get to enjoy the sight of the rich vegetation, wetlands and waterfalls, but also find out about the history of the region. Highlights include Jacks Hut, an old roadman's cottage, and the Dobson Memorial, a tall obelisk for Arthur Dudley Dobson, the original surveyor who gave the village and national park their names. *Difficulty: Medium • Time required: 3 hours return (can also be done one way if you drive or hitchhike back) • Follow signs from the car park up Punchbowl Road, or start at the Temple Basin car park up the other end (north from the village)*

Budget food

The village is very small, so there are few places to eat out at on a budget. In the village Challenge Arthur's Pass Cafe and Store is the cheapest place to go if you want to eat out and also sells some basic food and travel items (8am-5pm). Across the road Wobbly Kea has light meals and snacks for $6-$14, but main meals are rather expensive (10am-10pm). It's best to bring food with you from your last destination, such as Greymouth or Christchurch.

Recommended cheap accommodation

YHA Arthur's Pass (Mountain House)
All the facilities you would expect from a YHA hostel, from free wifi to well-cleaned rooms. *Dorm beds from $34, private rooms from $94 (10% off for YHA members) • Tel: 03 318 9258 • 84 West Coast Road, Arthur's Pass Village •* www.yha.co.nz

The Sanctuary Backpackers (BBH)
A short walk from the train station and coach drop off point, this hostel has a comfy lounge and central heating during winter. Note sleeping bags are required for the dorm rooms. Tent sites are also available for $10. *Beds from $26 for BBH members, from $30 for non-members • Tel: 027 466 2755 • 126 Main Road, Arthur's Pass Village •* www.thesanctuary.co.nz

How to get there and away

By bus

Atomic Travel (www.atomictravel.co.nz) have a shuttle service between Greymouth (1-2 hours, $40) and Christchurch (2-3 hours, $40). Sometimes a little cheaper is InterCity, but tickets are frequently sold out.

By car or campervan

Via State Highway 73, Arthur's Pass is just over one hour from Hokitika or Greymouth and almost two hours from Christchurch.

By train

The TranzAlpine train from Christchurch to Greymouth via Arthur's Pass is considered by many to be one of the most scenic train journeys in the world. Running once every day in both directions, it's a very relaxing way to see the mountain scenery, and also avoid the traffic. Trains from Christchurch (nearly 3 hours, $100-$140) and Greymouth (just over 2 hours, $100-$140) also have an open-air viewing platform. During non-peak seasons discounts are often advertised on the official website at www.greatjourneysofnz.co.nz/tranzalpine.

Some people have reported that cheaper tickets are available if booking from a New Zealand IP address (the computer's location), so if you do not see any 'Starter' fares or promotions, this may be worth investigating! One solution is to get someone you know in New Zealand to book for you. Alternatively you could use a VPN, which many people use to watch foreign TV that is not accessible where they live, to trick the system into believing you are in New Zealand. Of course you could just book when you arrive in New Zealand, but this risks prices going up before you book.

Tourist information

The Arthur's Pass Visitor Centre is located in the village center (8:30am-4:30pm), but your accommodation should also be a great place to ask if you have any questions.

Nelson

The oldest city in the South Island, Nelson is a compact town situated amid the amazing scenery of the Tasman Mountains. It's noted for its sunny climate, so you can come here pretty much any time of the year and expect good weather.

Things to do

Tahunanui Beach

This popular beach is a perfect spot for a swim, a relaxing stroll or a bit of sunbathing. While you can drive or take the bus, it's also worth considering cycling down the Rock Road, which makes for a very scenic bike ride. *By car: 10-minutes drive by car from central Nelson. By bus: take route 2 from the town center (adults $2.60, children $1.50)*

The center of New Zealand

Get a photo of yourself standing right bang in the center of New Zealand! It's a bit of a climb from the Botanical Reserve, but once you get to the top you'll be greeted with awesome views of the coastal town. *Difficulty: Medium • Time required: 30 minutes return • Trail starts towards the end of Hardy Street. It takes about 15 minutes on foot or a few minutes by car to get to the start*

Miyazu Japanese Garden

As anyone who has read Super Cheap Japan knows, spending a bit of time in a traditional Japanese garden is a great way to relax and clear your mind. This garden was built to celebrate Nelson and the Japanese town of Miyazu becoming sister towns. *FREE • 24h • By car: a few minutes north from the town. By bus: take route 1 from the town center (adults $2.60, children $1.50)*

Christ Church

This grand hilltop church, built in the 19th century, and its peaceful grounds, are worth a quick visit. *FREE • Opening times vary • Short walk south of the town center*

The Suter Art Gallery

Free gallery focusing on the works of 19th century artists, as well as temporary exhibitions from up-and-coming local ones. *FREE • 9:30am-4:30pm •* http://thesuter.org.nz *• Short walk from the town center (see map for directions)*

Founders Heritage Park

A wonderful collection of historic buildings. Some have little museums or shops inside, while there is also an organic brewery. Fun events are held for children and there is also a traditional railway experience on weekends (every day during school holidays). *Adults $7, children FREE • 10am-4:30pm •* www.founderspark.co.nz *• About five minutes on foot from Miyazu Japanese Garden. By car: several minutes north from the town. By bus: take route 1 from the town center (adults $2.60, children $1.50)*

Discount stores

The Warehouse is located next to the large Countdown on St Vincent Street (8am-10pm). Hello Banana (9am-6pm) and Two Dollar Things (9am-5:30pm) in the downtown area are well stocked with party goods and other variety items.

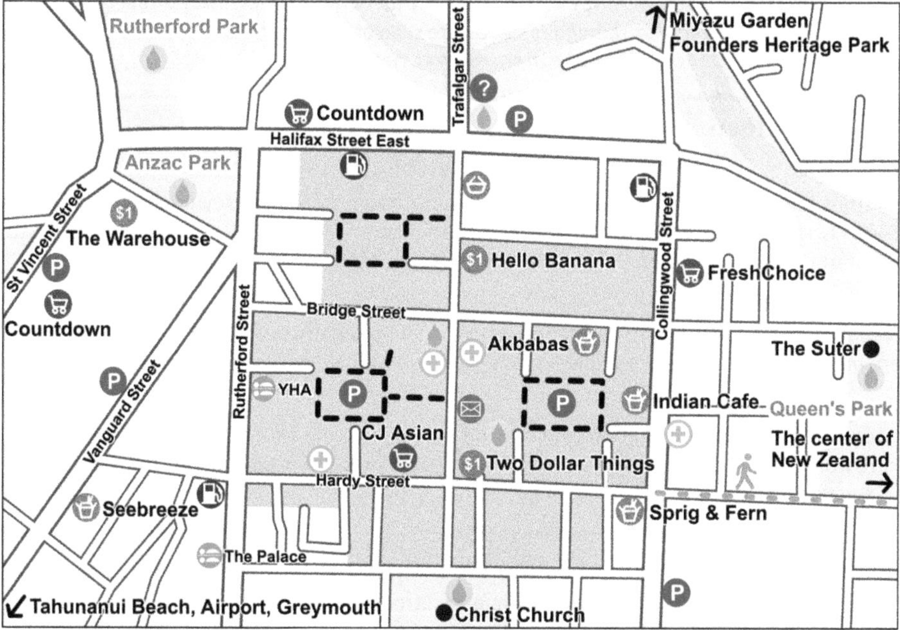

Budget food

Sprig & Fern - Check out the $10 lunch deals at this funky pub. Also a great way to try out local beers. *Meals from $10 • 11am-12am (2pm-12am on Sundays)*

Indian Cafe - Reasonably priced Indian restaurant with lunch deals and takeaway available. *Meals from $12 • 12pm-2pm, 5pm-9:30pm (not open for lunch on weekends)*

Akbabas - This popular kebab joint has decent portion sizes, as well as a wide selection of Turkish drinks and salads. *Meals $8-12 • 11am-9pm*

Seabreeze City Takeaways - Really cheap fish and chips. They also sell stuffed jacket potatoes, called spuds, which are excellent for a light meal or snack. *Meals from $5 • 4:30pm-8:30pm (until 8pm Sunday to Tuesday)*

Cheap supermarkets

Countdown have two stores in central Nelson, one on Halifax Street East (7am-10pm) and a much larger one a short walk away on St Vincent Street (7am-10pm). CJ Asian is also a good choice, especially if you have a hankering for healthy Asian food (9am-7pm).

Recommended cheap accommodation

Honeysuckle House (BBH)

Free airport pickups, bread, milk, ice cream, tea, coffee and bikes. In other words, this is a great place for penny-pinching backpackers! *Beds from $31 (from $27 with BBH card) • Tel: 03 548 7576 • 125 Tasman Street, Nelson •* https://honeysucklehouse.weebly.com

YHA Nelson

Very professionally run hostel in the heart of town, with two kitchens and a large lounge. *Beds from $19 (10% off for YHA members) • Tel: 03 545 9988 • 59 Rutherford Street, Nelson •* www.yha.co.nz

The Palace Backpackers (BBH)

Fun, super friendly hostel with free breakfasts. They don't have bunks, just normal beds, so you'll also probably get a better night's sleep here than at most hostels. *Beds from $28 (from $24 with BBH card) • Tel: 03 548 4691 • 114 Rutherford Street, Nelson •* www.thepalace.co.nz

---

How to get there and away

By bus

InterCity stops off here, with coaches from Picton (2 hours, $23) and Greymouth (6 hours, $40). Kiwi Experience and Stray also go here on their routes. Nelson Lake Shuttles run buses to the start of nearby hiking trails (www.nelsonlakesshuttles.co.nz).

By car or campervan

Nelson is two hours from Picton and four hours from Greymouth via State Highway 6. There are plenty of gas stations around town, so fill up here before heading off.

By air

Budget airline Jetstar flies here from Auckland or Wellington, with Air New Zealand also flying here from Christchurch. Super Shuttles (www.supershuttle.co.nz) provide bus transportation to and from the airport.

Tourist information

There is a tourist information center on Trafalgar Street (10am-4pm).

Many thanks for reading

Help spread the word!

Please help this self-published book by writing a review on the website where you bought the book, sharing the book on Facebook, Twitter or Instagram, or telling a friend. As this is a self-funded indie project, it would be super useful and very much appreciated!

Like or follow us to get the latest tips and deals

Join or follow Super Cheap Guides to get the latest information on new discounts and deals, plus interesting budget travel reports. You can also head to the website to read all the latest information or get it sent straight to your inbox by signing up for the free newsletter.

 **www.supercheapguides.com**

 **@SuperCheapGuides**

 **@SuperCheapGuides**

 **@SuperCheapGuide**

Picture Attribution

Also available from Super Cheap Guides

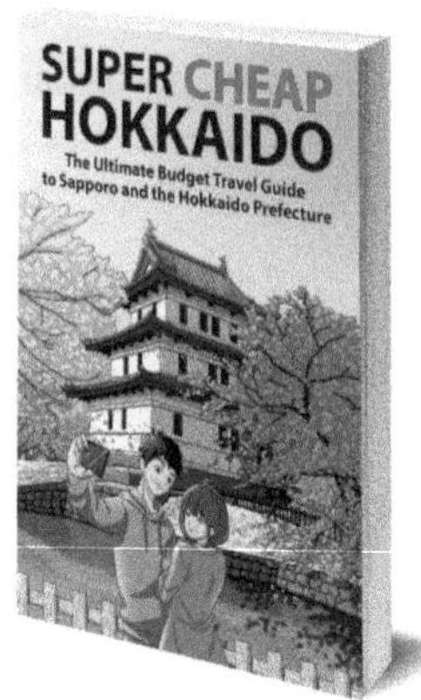

Super Cheap Japan: Budget Travel in Tokyo, Kyoto, Osaka, Nara, Hiroshima and Surrounding Areas (ISBN: 978-1-9998100-0-9)

The ultimate budget travel guide to a cheap holiday in Honshu (Japan's main island). Go shopping for $4 clothes in Tokyo, enjoy inexpensive hikes in Nikko, or visit Kyoto's beautiful shrines and gardens on the cheap; all with this super helpful guide.

Super Cheap Tokyo: The Ultimate Budget Travel Guide to Tokyo and the Kanto Region (ISBN: 978-1-9998100-5-4)

Super Cheap Tokyo is all you'll need for budget holiday in Tokyo and the surrounding Kanto region. Buy clothes in fashion heaven Harajuku for under $10, spend next to nothing on a day's hiking or relax in a free Japanese garden; it's all here in this easy-to-use travel guide.

Super Cheap Hokkaido: The Ultimate Budget Travel Guide to Sapporo and the Hokkaido Prefecture (ISBN: 978-1-9131140-0-8)

The perfect companion for a budget holiday to Sapporo and the surrounding Hokkaido prefecture. A follow-up to the bestselling Super Cheap Japan guidebook, this book will show you exactly how, where and when you can save money on your trip.

Check out www.supercheapguides.com for more information!

Please only buy authentic books from Super Cheap Guides to avoid disappointment. All our books are authored by Matthew Baxter, under the Super Cheap Japan or Super Cheap Guides publisher names.

About the Author

Super Cheap New Zealand was written by Matthew Baxter, a British travel author who lived in New Zealand for many years. Having traveled across the country, without much money, he has built up an extensive knowledge of budget travel in this beautiful land, and also worked at many leading tourism companies there. He previously wrote the best-selling guidebook Super Cheap Japan and also writes professionally for several websites and publications, such as the GaijinPot, All About and the Japan National Tourist Association.